How to Complete Your UCAS Application

2019 Entry

Beryl Dixon and UCAS

30th edition

Getting into guides

Getting into Art & Design Courses, 10th edition
Getting into Business & Economics Courses, 12th edition
Getting into Dental School, 10th edition
Getting into Engineering Courses, 4th edition
Getting into Law, 12th edition
Getting into Medical School 2019 Entry, 23rd edition
Getting into Oxford & Cambridge 2019 Entry, 21st edition
Getting into Pharmacy and Pharmacology Courses, 2nd edition
Getting into Physiotherapy Courses, 9th edition
Getting into Psychology Courses, 12th edition
Getting into Veterinary School, 11th edition
How to Complete Your UCAS Application 2019 Entry, 30th edition

How to Complete Your UCAS Application 2019 Entry

This 30th edition published in 2018 by Trotman Education, an imprint of Crimson Publishing Ltd, 21d Charles Street, Bath BA1 1HX.

© Crimson Publishing Ltd 2018

Authors: Beryl Dixon and UCAS

Foreword by Fatuma Mahad © Fatuma Mahad

Screenshots from UCAS Apply, Figures 1 and 2 © UCAS. Reproduced with kind permission of UCAS.

British Library Cataloguing in Publication Data
A catalogue record for this book is available from the British Library

ISBN 978 1 911067 86 3

Printed and bound in Malta by Gutenberg Press Ltd

Contents

Contents

Foreword

First decision: where to begin?

Congratulations! You've made an important decision to apply for a university or college course. With so many choices to make you might need some help in deciding what and where to study. This book will guide you to information to help you turn that decision into a reality.

As well as supporting the whole application process, UCAS helps thousands of potential students find the right study match. We believe that giving you access to as much information as possible at this stage in your application is vital in ensuring that you make the right decisions about your future study.

The research you do and the advice you get can provide a valuable insight into which course is perfect for you. Our UCAS search tool on www.ucas.com is the definitive source of information on courses of higher education and universities. We advise you to look closely at this information, be realistic about entry requirements and, if possible, make a visit to the universities and colleges that you are interested in. Remember, you could potentially be spending three or four years there, so it needs to feel like the right place for you.

You'll find www.ucas.com has all the information you need to help you make your application. There are downloads, guides and how-to videos, as well as plenty of tips and blogs from students, parents and advisers. Have a look around – and talk to us on Facebook or Twitter if you've got any questions.

The actual process of applying is simple and is all online. You can find everything you need to know about it in this book, but if you have a question that remains unanswered, contact us online or call one of our experts.

Best of luck with your research and application!

Fatuma Mahad
Director of Technology and Operations, UCAS

Introduction

This book is intended to be a guide for anyone wanting to gain a place on a UK higher education course. In 2017, 699,850 people applied for courses through UCAS – almost unchanged from the previous year – and 533,890 people were accepted on to courses of higher education at 375 UK universities and colleges. For 2018, by the main application deadline of 15 January 2018, 559,000 people had made applications through UCAS, a decrease of 0.9% compared to the same point last year. The number of applicants will almost certainly increase over the year since many people, particularly international students, apply after the 'advisory' January deadline. (On average over 3% of all applications to UCAS are made after the January deadline has expired.) All of these potential students had to complete UCAS applications to try to gain their university or college place.

The job of UCAS

With very few exceptions, every application to a full-time higher educa-tion course, whether a degree, a course leading to a degree, a founda-tion degree, Higher National Diploma (HND) or Diploma of Higher Education (DipHE), must be made through UCAS. UCAS manages and monitors the flow of applications to universities and colleges and their decisions to would-be entrants. UCAS acts as the intermediary between students and their intended universities and colleges, providing lists of available courses and the means by which prospective students can apply for them.

As well as handling initial applications, UCAS also offers two valuable services when the summer exam results come out: Adjustment and Clearing. Both services are designed to help students whose results are not what they expected (Adjustment for those with better grades and Clearing for those whose grades are lower). Both services are described in Chapter 10.

UCAS offers a considerable amount of help to higher education appli-cants on its website, www.ucas.com, where you can:

- use the UCAS search tool to research the courses offered by dif-ferent universities and colleges using a number of variables, such as qualification (degree, HND, etc.), subject, university or college, or geographical area

- find out the entry requirements for courses, including grades and Tariff* points and any additional requirements
- find out more about each course, including its content, teaching methods and method of assessment, all in the course details
- link to any higher education institution's website
- make an online application to your chosen university courses through Apply*
- log in to Track* to follow the progress of your application
- link to Extra* to find an additional course to apply to, if you have used all your choices and are not holding any offers
- get information about financing your studies
- go through Clearing if you have your results but no offers.

* All these terms are explained in the Glossary (see page 167).

Of course, applying through UCAS is no guarantee of a place on a higher education course. Every year, a number of people apply but are not offered places.

Using this guide

This book is divided into three parts. A brief outline of the content and purpose of each part is given below.

Part I. In the think tank

Before you make a UCAS application, it is important that you thoroughly research all your higher education options. The first part of this guide gives you a number of ideas about the areas you need to consider carefully before you can be confident of making the right higher education course choices. Its six chapters guide you through the decision-making process, helping you to find answers to key questions such as these:

- Is higher education the right option for me? (See Chapter 1)
- How will a degree or higher diploma fit in with my career plans? (See Chapter 2)
- How will I afford it? (See Chapter 3)
- How do I choose what and where to study? (See Chapters 4 and 5)
- Will I meet the entry requirements? (See Chapter 6.)

You need to be ready to explain and justify your decision. Admissions tutors (who read your UCAS application and who may interview you) will want to know why you have applied for a place on their particular course. At the end of most chapters there is a 'Resources' section suggesting points of reference that can be accessed in your school or college library or local careers centre. Ask advisers for help in finding the most up-to-date materials.

Part II. The admissions procedure: applications, interviews, offers and beyond

Once you have decided which courses to apply for, the second part of the book gives you an overview of the entire admissions procedure. It works through the whole process, answering key questions such as these:

- When do I submit my application? (See Chapter 7)
- How do universities and colleges communicate their offers to me? (See Chapter 7)
- How do I accept or decline offers? (See Chapter 7)
- What about non-standard applications? (See Chapter 8)
- How can I maximise my chances if I'm called for interview? (See Chapter 9)
- What happens on exam results day? (See Chapter 10)
- How do I use Clearing? (See Chapter 10)

Part III. Using Apply to submit your UCAS application

Part III covers the technicalities of filling in and submitting your UCAS application online using Apply, taking you through the process step by step and offering helpful advice and tips on how to avoid the pitfalls.

Staying on the straight and narrow: timetable for advanced-level students

If you stick to the timetable, the whole process of applying to higher education is straightforward. The application timetable below will give you an idea of what you should be doing and when. Refer to the relevant chapters for further information.

(Note: the term advanced-level students does not mean simply A level students – it is for all students doing any advanced or level 3 course.)

First year of advanced-level course

Autumn term

- Start to explore the range of possible options beyond your advanced-level courses at school or college (see Chapters 1 and 2).
- Consider your GCSE or equivalent qualifications – the range and grades achieved – and review any A level, Scottish Higher, International Baccalaureate (IB), Irish Leaving Certificate (ILC) or BTEC National subjects that you are taking (see Chapter 6).
- Will your qualifications enable you to fulfil your future plans? Discuss this point with your careers adviser.

Spring term

- Work through a skills, aptitudes and interests guide, such as Centigrade or Morrisby, or complete a career development profiling exercise (see Chapter 2).
- Start to research your higher education options in the light of these results. Prepare for and attend a UCAS higher education exhibition (see Chapters 4 and 5).
- Explore the financial implications of attending a higher education course (see Chapter 3).

Summer term

- Prepare for and attend a UCAS exhibition, if you missed out on this in the spring (see Chapters 4 and 5).
- Attend university and college open days.
- Continue to research your higher education options, checking UCAS course requirements and entry profiles.
- Draw up a shortlist of possible universities and/or colleges.
- Make decisions on courses and modules to take next year.
- Arrange to do work experience during the summer. To have done this is important for entry to some courses, for example medicine, those leading to healthcare professions (such as occupational therapy, physiotherapy, radiography and speech therapy), veterinary science and veterinary medicine, social work, the land-based industries and teaching degree courses (see Chapter 2).
- Try to obtain sponsorship for courses – write to possible organisations you have researched (see Chapter 3).
- Start to organise your year out if you plan to take a gap year.
- Gather up material evidence from which to draft a personal statement for your UCAS application (see Chapter 17).
- Research details for sitting the UK Clinical Aptitude Test (UKCAT), which is required for entry to medicine and dentistry at some universities. You may register from 9am on 1 May until 5pm on 18 September and take the test between 2 July and 2 October. The fee is lower in July and August. (See Chapter 9.)

Summer holidays

- Undertake the work experience you arranged during the summer term. Keep a diary of what you did so that you can refer back to it when writing your personal statement (see Chapter 17).
- Possibly attend a taster course (arranged by many universities). More on this in Chapter 4.

Second year of advanced-level course

Autumn term

- Between 5 September and 15 January – preferably as early as possible – submit your completed UCAS application using Apply (see Chapter 7 and Part III).

- If you need to take the Law National Aptitude Test (LNAT), which is required by most universities, you may register from 1 August and may take the test after 1 September. The standard closing date is 20 January but some universities have an earlier date (see Chapter 9).
- Between 1 September and 1 October arrange to take the BMAT – BioMedical Admissions Test (see Chapter 9) – if necessary, for a 31 October test date. (Late entry fees apply after 15 October.)
- Before 2 October take the UKCAT test if necessary.
- Before 15 October (18.00 hours UK time), submit your UCAS application for the universities of Oxford and Cambridge. If you are applying to Cambridge from outside the EU or you wish to be considered for an organ scholarship, you must submit a Cambridge Online Preliminary Application (COPA) form as well as a UCAS application. UK and other EU applicants do not need to do this. Applicants for the University of Oxford are not required to submit a separate application form but extra information is required for some international interviews and for choral or organ awards (see Chapter 8 and Part III).
- Before 15 October (18.00 hours UK time), submit all UCAS applications for entry to medicine, dentistry, veterinary science and veterinary medicine.

Spring term
- 15 January (18.00 hours UK time) is the application deadline for UCAS to receive applications for all courses except those with a 15 October deadline and art and design courses with a 24 March deadline. Visit the UCAS search tool at www.ucas.com to find out whether your chosen art and design courses have a 15 January or 24 March deadline.
- Apply for bursaries, sponsorship or scholarships as appropriate.
- Prepare for possible interviews with admissions tutors; a mock interview if your school/college offers them is useful at this point.
- If you live in England, Wales and Northern Ireland, you should make your application for financial assessment through the Student Loans Company, whatever your particular circumstances. Applicants from Scotland make their application for financial assessment to the Student Awards Agency for Scotland (SAAS).
- From 25 February, if you used all five choices in your application but are not holding an offer of a place, you can use the Extra option.
- 24 March (18.00 hours UK time) is the application deadline for the receipt at UCAS of applications for art and design courses (except those listed with a 15 January deadline).
- By 31 March, universities and colleges are advised to send UCAS their decisions on all applications received by the 15 January deadline. (Their absolute deadline to inform UCAS of their decisions is 2 May.)

Summer term

- By 2 May, decisions should have been received from all universities and colleges.
- If you receive all your university and college decisions by 2 May, you should reply to any offers by 6 June.
- Before 30 June, further applications can be made using UCAS Extra (if you applied for five courses originally and are not holding an offer); 30 June (18.00 hours UK time) is the last date for receipt of all applications before Clearing.

Summer holidays

- 5 July is IB results day; 15 August is results day for A levels; results of Scottish Highers will be released on 7 August. If you have met all the conditions of your firm choice and exceeded at least one of these, you will be eligible to register to look for another course during the Adjustment period.
- UCAS Clearing vacancy information is available from the beginning of July. If you don't get the results you were hoping for, you may need additional support through Clearing to find an alternative higher education option or further information and guidance from your local careers service.
- 20 September is the last date for Clearing applications.

Part I
In the think tank

1 | Is higher education right for you?

Overview of higher education today

Applying for entry to higher education may well be the most important step that you've taken up to now. It's one that will certainly affect the next three or more years of your life and in the long term will affect your career choices and prospects, which in turn will impact on your future lifestyle.

There are plenty of individuals to consult to help you choose your higher education course and place of study – your careers adviser, your careers and subject teachers, your present employer, your parents (throughout this book, the term 'parents' should be read to mean parents or legal guardians), your partner and wider family and friends. But the decision is ultimately yours and, since it will affect your life for several years to come, you need to be confident about the suitability of your chosen higher education course.

Every year, people take up places only to find that the course content, teaching style or institution is not what they expected – and they subsequently leave their courses. The average non-continuation rate during the first year of study on a full-time first degree course is, according to the Higher Education Statistics Agency, 6.4%, but the rate at individual universities and colleges varies considerably. For instance at 29 institutions the non-continuation rate is 10% or higher, at four it rises to over 16%, whereas 12 are at 2% or under (source: Higher Education Statistics Agency 2018, first degree courses, UK-domiciled students only).

This can be difficult, not just for the student but also for the university or college, so it is worth taking the time at this stage to make sure that your application choices are really appropriate for you.

All about you

Before considering higher education courses, there are a few points on which you really need to know your own mind. Take a look at the questions in the following paragraphs and work out where you stand.

Are you happy to continue in education, full or part time, for a further two, three or four years?

Going on to higher education is a big step to take. Put simply, you've got to be committed and enthusiastic. If you do not enjoy your chosen course, you will find your time in higher education very difficult.

Advanced-level study – for example GCE, A level, Scottish Higher, Irish Leaving Certificate (ILC), International Baccalaureate (IB), BTEC National Award and so on – is an essential preparation for many aspects of higher education, not just in terms of subject-specific knowledge but also in terms of analytical skills. On your higher education course, you will be developing your powers of deduction, reasoning, critical analysis and evaluation just as much as you will be learning new facts about your chosen subject. Are you ready for this?

There are literally thousands of courses that are not straight developments of school- or college-based study – many are fascinating and worthwhile combinations that include opportunities for studying abroad. Does the thought of all this fill you with excitement or leave you pretty cold?

Do you have a strong and ongoing interest in self-development?

Your friends may already have started earning and could become more independent while you continue to study and accumulate sizeable debts. Can you be patient and philosophical, anticipating an interesting career and a better standard of living as an experienced graduate?

Do people around you (family, friends, girlfriend or boyfriend) appreciate and support your intention to continue your education? If they do not, do you anticipate that this will pose practical or emotional challenges for you? And if they do, will they be as understanding and continue to value and support you in two or three years' time?

Have you the necessary sticking power if others withdraw their support?

Have you seriously explored your aptitudes, interests and career aspirations?

Do you want to learn more because you have strong ability in a particular area and because you find the subject matter interesting? If so, you are in a good starting position and are likely to enjoy your studies.

Some degree-level courses explore one particular subject area in great depth, with no obvious link to employment or a career structure (for example history, anthropology, geography, physics, English, American studies and French). Have you thought about what you will do once you graduate? How will your degree link with your long-term career plan?

(See Chapter 2 for more on this.) A degree may only be a stepping stone to the start of a professional career – once you are in employment, it is often necessary to continue studying to gain professional qualifications. You will need commitment!

Some people are influenced by promotional publicity or by the enthusiasm of other people and do not consider the possible long-term impact of their choice on themselves. You need to think carefully about this.

Step back and try a number of aptitude and interest guides that are available online and in careers centres (see the 'Resources' section at the end of Chapter 2). You need to investigate the values and attitudes needed to strengthen your decision making.

Are you ready to be a student?

Student life is likely to offer you all of the social and extracurricular opportunities you ever dreamed of – are you confident that you will be able to balance your social life with your studies, particularly if you apply for a course with fewer scheduled contact hours such as English or history? Remember, there is a big change from the guided learning you have experienced at school or college to the self-management of study in higher education.

You will have to develop your own study skills and become an independent, self-motivated learner. Your subject teachers or tutors can offer helpful guidance on this point.

Do not be surprised if you feel confused and uncertain about applying to courses a long way from home. You are taking an important decision that may result in you striking out on your own, seemingly leaving behind everything you find familiar. It's natural to feel apprehensive about this – many people do experience insecurity and can feel isolated and disorientated at first, but most find they adapt very quickly.

If you are feeling very worried about the prospect of leaving home, talk to a friendly careers adviser, student adviser, personal tutor, or a friend or relative, and focus on the positive aspects of your higher education intentions. It is important to make sure you are clear about your plans and the changes these will mean for your day-to-day life.

Lastly – money. How you are going to finance your higher education course is likely to be a major consideration. You will need to give careful thought to the financial implications of going through higher education. For example, some people decide to live at home rather than go away in order to save money. Some make their choice from universities and colleges that offer cheaper accommodation. Others look carefully at the scholarships and bursaries on offer at different places. This subject is discussed in depth in Chapter 3.

Conclusion

The decision to pursue a higher education course is not one that should be taken lightly. However, if you have read through the questions and points above and still feel confident that higher education is the right choice for you, read on. The rest of Part I will help you focus your research so that you can cut down the huge number of courses on offer to the five you will enter on your UCAS application.

As you work through the following chapters, keep testing yourself by asking the following questions.

- Have I given enough consideration to this point?
- Which resources proved useful in my research?
- Have I talked to people with knowledge or experience in this area?
- Will I feel the same in two or three years' time?

Should I do more research?

Essential research

- Talk to subject teachers, tutors or form teachers and careers advisers.
- Check to see whether your local careers service gives information on higher education opportunities on its website.
- Use the timetable on pages 3 to 6 to draw up your own calendar of important dates and deadlines. You will need to make decisions about courses to apply to in the autumn term of 2018, and all subsequent UCAS deadlines must then be met.

2 | Looking to the future: career routes

Since you will be committing a lot of time and money to following a higher education course, it is vital to have researched possible career routes leading on from graduation. This is the moment for in-depth careers exploration and planning, looking at where a particular subject area might take you and also at what previous graduates have gone on to do.

This may seem very difficult. How can you possibly know yet what you want to do in four or more years' time? How can you ever narrow down the options when you are having enough trouble just choosing which courses to apply for? Some people, of course, do have firm career ideas. For others this idea of planning for the future can be difficult to face because it may seem that there is simply too much choice. It may also seem time consuming when you are busy working for exams.

Investigating possible careers does not, in most cases, mean committing yourself to one particular one at this stage. An important thing to remember is that any decisions you make or ideas you have at this stage are not set in stone. You can change and adapt your plans as you go along. It is good to have some career ideas though, not least because admissions tutors want to know that you are looking ahead, and that you are going to be an interested and motivated student with a career development plan that extends well beyond your time at university or college. If you are called to interview (see Chapter 9), having thought your plans through will mean you aren't floored by any career-related questions.

There are many people who can help you form some ideas about a future career but, if available, your first port of call should be the school/college's careers department or a discussion with a careers adviser. Ask at your school or college whether this is possible. Unfortunately provision for this varies in different areas but there are other people you can ask for help – parents, friends, former students from your school or college – and there are useful IT programs which your school or college might have. These are listed at the end of the chapter.

Developing a career plan

If you already have a career plan

If you already have a particular career in mind, now is the time to research it in as much depth as possible. Find out which courses are the most relevant, which get you professional accreditation in the career you have chosen (if applicable) – for many careers a degree is only the first step and you will have to undertake further training, often in employ-ment, in order to qualify; examples include accountancy and engineer-ing. Find out, too, which have the best record of placing graduates in their chosen career area. For more on this, see Chapters 4 and 5.

If you already know what subject interests you, but you do not know what you want to do next

This is the time to do some broad research. Take a look at a careers directory or website (see the 'Resources' section at the end of this chapter) to find out what's out there, and focus on the jobs that seem to relate to your chosen subject. Research possible progression routes and projected salaries in different careers. If you are interested in a career that requires postgraduate training in order to qualify with a professional association you should look on the organisation's website to find out what will be required after your degree. You could also inves-tigate future job opportunities and likely salaries. If you are interested in a subject that does not lead directly to a specific career, for example history or sociology, a good starting point is to find out which careers have been entered by graduates in these subjects. This information is usually available on universities' and colleges' websites. Find the sub-ject department and look up destinations of recent graduates. It will also be useful to find out how many of last year's graduates are in full-time professional occupations drawing on their particular skills and abilities.

In addition to looking at universities' and colleges' own websites, you could consult the latest edition of *What Do Graduates Do?* which is jointly produced by the Higher Education Careers Services Unit (HECSU) and the Association of Graduate Careers Advisory Services (AGCAS). The report, which gives the destinations of students who graduated in 2017 six months after graduation, is available at www.hecsu.ac.uk.

Better still, try to find information on graduates' destinations one or two years on, if universities and colleges are able to provide this. They are required by the government to provide figures after six months, but this information is not particularly valuable because many graduates are in temporary employment at this stage while earning money to pay off debts or go travelling, or they are still in the process of applying for permanent jobs. Again, the websites of individual subject departments could be useful here. (And if they have former students who are in particularly interesting jobs, you can be sure that the information will be there!)

If you have no idea at all

If you're not sure what subject area interests you and you do not have a particular career in mind, it may be worth reconsidering whether higher education is really the right choice for you. On the other hand, if you are simply feeling bewildered by the number of options available to you, there are plenty of books, websites and IT programs that can help you to assess your interests. Try a range of them, and take it from there.

> **TIP!**
>
> Remember – your careers adviser is always a good starting point.

The graduate skill set

Some courses lead naturally into a recognised career or occupational area (for example engineering, hospitality management, law and medicine), but most do not. For most people, therefore, the value of higher education in terms of career prospects is that it enables you to develop a 'graduate skill set', because study of any subject at this level should develop your abilities in some of the areas regarded as important by employers, while other opportunities available in higher education can help you to develop other, equally valuable, skills.

The Right Combination, Education and Skills Survey, published by the CBI (Confederation of British Industry) and Pearson Education, reports views from employers on which skills are important for people leaving higher education to possess.

'Graduates' attitudes matter most of all to recruiters …

'The reality for graduates is that simply gaining a degree is not enough to win entry to a successful career. Despite the growing demand for graduate-level skills, there will always be tough competition among candidates for prime graduate appointments. Developing the right skills and attitudes is critically important for a successful transition from higher education to the world of work.

'When selecting graduate recruits, businesses look first and foremost for the attitudes and aptitudes that will enable them to be effective in the workplace.

'Year after year, this is by far the most widely cited consideration among graduate recruiters. Nearly nine in ten employers (87%) this year identify it as among their three most important factors and it far outranks all others.'

Reproduced with kind permission.
If interested, you can read the survey in full at
www.cbi.org.uk/cbi-prod/assets/File/pdf/cbi-education-and-skills-survey2016.pdf.

Attitude and aptitude for work. What are these skills?

They are often known as non-technical, soft, transferable or employ-ability skills.

They have different names in different organisations but they generally come under the following headings:

- business and customer awareness
- communication and literacy
- critical thinking
- entrepreneurship/enterprise
- IT
- managing complex information
- numeracy
- positive attitude
- problem solving
- research skills
- self-management
- team working.

To quote from another important organisation – Stephen Isherwood, Chief Executive of the Association of Graduate Recruiters, an organisation representing over 700 employers, says:

'Employers want to hire graduates with a mix of knowledge, skills and abilities plus a meaningful interest in the work that they do. The language will differ from employer to employer but essentially employers seek those with:

- people skills to get work done with others
- practical intelligence to solve problems
- resilience to deal with difficult situations
- flexibility to deal with change
- self-awareness to keep developing as a person
- drive and motivation to do the job.

'All of these attributes you will hone on the job, but to get the job you need to show your potential. That can be done through work experience, internships, volunteering and part-time jobs as long as you reflect on your experiences and articulate your abilities through the application process.'

Many degree and diploma programmes do not at first sight appear to develop such skills. But you could be surprised! If you check your chosen course at several different universities and colleges, using the UCAS search tool (more on this at the end of Chapter 4), and look at individual colleges and universities' entries, you will find the skills that they view as being provided by each of their programmes. The careers advisory services may also be able to assist. They are there to help students in all years, and making early contact can be very profitable.

Some universities and colleges include relevant modules in all their courses and issue students with a logbook or certificate that shows how they gained each skill – for example:

- analysis and solving problems
- team working and interpersonal skills
- verbal communication
- written communication
- personal planning and organising
- initiative
- numerical reasoning
- information literacy and IT.

The above is not the case in all universities and colleges, but many careers services or employability centres now run separate employability and personal development courses which you may follow at the same time as you work for your academic qualifications. These courses are well worth exploring when you arrive at university or college – and it's even more worthwhile if you sign up for them! You will normally receive an award that will be understood by many graduate employers who will be familiar with its content.

Many careers advisory services also run special sessions for students to help them understand which transferable skills are most in demand by employers and how to acquire them. Some workshops are run by major employers in conjunction with careers advisory services; others are run independently by careers advisers and focus on subjects such as:

- assessment centres
- commercial awareness
- numbers for the world of work (designed to give confidence in numeracy)
- how to raise your profile when networking online
- industry insights
- marvellous meetings
- perfect presentations
- realise your strengths
- interview skills
- preparing for psychometric assessment
- project management

- putting your skills to work
- success in business
- team and leadership development.

Having high-level skills in these areas will increase your appeal to prospective employers, which is essential in the present climate. With severe competition for the best graduate jobs, employers are able to pick and choose. You might like to see what is offered in the way of employability skills training before you make your final choice of course and university or college.

However, as stated earlier, some university and college admissions tutors – and some graduate employers – will also require you to have demonstrated your interest in your chosen career area through work experience or work placements *before you apply for a higher education place through UCAS*. This is a major reason why it is important to think hard about your career aspirations as early as possible.

Work experience

Now

Being able to write about suitable work experience on your UCAS form will, for many courses, boost your application. Many courses (those linked with health or social care and with careers in the land-based industries, for example) nearly always expect applicants to have arranged some experience – even for a short period – in a relevant job. Maybe your school or college is already on to this and has arranged some form of work experience or shadowing for you. If not, you could try to arrange something yourself to take place in the holidays.

Even one or two days spent in gaining relevant experience or in work shadowing can be helpful.

What is work shadowing?

This term refers to observing someone at work – normally in a highly skilled job. A solicitor, dentist or surgeon for instance might let a student spend some time with them but they could hardly expect to try out the job! A good shadowing period would though allow for explanations and answering questions.

Try some or all of the following:

- look for the type of business you'd like to work for (for example, solicitors, hospitals, etc.)
- make a list of the companies you'd like to work for
- make a note of their phone numbers and addresses – you can usually get these details online

- ask if they have any work experience opportunities by letter or email; it is a good idea to phone first and ask who would be the appropriate person to contact.

If they don't have any opportunities at the time, you could ask if they could contact you when something comes up next – and offer to send them a copy of your CV (a document that lists your personal information, education and experience; this is sometimes also known as a résumé, though this is primarily a North American term).

Writing a CV

A CV should include:

- your full name
- postal address
- contact details – telephone number and email address
- education – schools/colleges, qualifications obtained, beginning with ones obtained most recently
- skills e.g. knowledge of computer/software packages, driving licence
- previous work experience, giving name of employers
- positions of responsibility in school or college, positions of responsibility held in your own time
- interests/hobbies
- names of two or three referees – people who can provide a reference.

A CV should be word processed on plain paper and should not be more than two sides in length.

You should send an accompanying letter with it.

You must get permission to give people's names as referees.

A sample CV

Rebecca Alice Johnson

Address: 5 Kestrel Crescent, Anytown, Wiltshire, SP9 8QZ.

Email: raj99@blankmail.co.uk

Date of Birth: 23 March 2002.

Nationality: British.

Education
2013–2019 Anytown High School.

2019 A levels to be taken: French, History, Mathematics.

2017: GCSEs: English (7), Biology (C), Business Studies (B), Chemistry (A), French (A), Geography (A), German (A), History (A), Mathematics (7), Physics (B).

Work Experience:
2017–2018 Saturday sales assistant in Barkers Shoes. My duties include moving stock from the store room to the sales floor, operating the till and advising customers. The role requires accuracy and good communication skills.

Skills:
Good spoken and written French and German.
Good keyboard skills and knowledge of Excel and PowerPoint.
Driving licence.

Positions of Responsibility
Captain of school hockey team, Chairman of school debating society, Assistant Leader of Brownies.

Interests
Music (grade 6 clarinet), cinema, theatre and swimming.

Referees
Mrs H Mills, Brownie pack leader; Mr F King, Manager, Barkers Shoes. Details available on request.

Finding work experience isn't always possible, however. Some professionals, such as doctors, vets, accountants and lawyers, are often flooded with requests from students. In addition they have the problem of contacting patients or clients to ask if they will agree to have a student present.

If you cannot get any experience in the profession you are hoping to enter, there are alternatives. You could, for example, visit law courts and observe different kinds of trial. If you cannot arrange work experience in a hospital or with a GP, you could try to observe what goes on at a typical doctor's practice. You could ask if it is possible to spend some time with a practice nurse or healthcare assistant.

If you cannot find any opportunities in a relevant profession, you could still demonstrate that you have the right sort of personal skills by doing paid or voluntary work in a caring environment where you will learn to work with people directly, for example:

- in a children's nursery if you are interested in teaching
- in a day centre for people with disabilities if nursing, physiotherapy or social work interests you
- with a volunteer agency such as a drug rehabilitation centre or a night shelter for homeless people if you hope to study social work or psychology

- on a local conservation project if you are hoping to do a course connected with the environment.

While you should not do voluntary work just to make your UCAS application look good, it can certainly help strengthen an application. However, more importantly it can give you the satisfaction of helping other people and help you to find out a bit more about careers that might interest you. A good place to start is your local volunteer centre, which will have a list of opportunities, or through online databases such as www.do-it.org, where you can search for over one million volunteering opportunities by interest, activity or location and apply online.

Describing your work experience on your UCAS application

'If you have done any work experience that is relevant to the course you are applying for, use this to help your application. However, don't go into too much detail about what you did, but use the experience to reflect on the time spent there and what you gained from it. What did you learn that was relevant to the subject? Did the experience help you to clarify your choice of degree or career? What did you learn about yourself as a person? What skills did you acquire? Say what skills you now realise you need to develop and explain how the course you are applying for will help you to gain them.

'If you have no recent work experience you might want to reflect on your Year 10 experience and think about that. Although at first it might not seem relevant to you, any experience of work can be used to show how you have gained transferable skills like communication and acceptance of responsibility.

'Remember throughout your personal statement to REFLECT on your experiences and skills and always try to RELATE them to your chosen course.'

Advice from Alison Wilson, Schools and Colleges Liaison
Coordinator, University of Winchester

While in higher education

The same points apply once you get to university or college. You will probably need to work during term time, so look first for relevant experience. Try to spend time in a job that will broaden your experience and give you insight into a potential employment area. If that is not possible, do your best to draw up a list of soft skills applicable to any career that you have acquired from experience in any kind of job – bar work, sales … whatever you can find.

Your university's careers advisory service or student services unit can usually help and may run a job shop especially to find part-time opportunities for students. It can also provide details of vacation work placements – and may even be able to give you a grant to help with additional expenses you might incur on a placement.

TIP!

Admissions tutors are impressed by applicants who have built up knowledge of a related work sector and whose plans include developing useful employment links while studying.

If you have really tried hard to obtain work experience but have been unsuccessful, explain this on your UCAS application and describe the related activities that you have undertaken as an alternative.

Case study

Georgia Everall graduated from York University with a degree in psychology.

She now works for a charity in York which is a partnership of the city's leading employers committed to making York a better place through employee-volunteering – for example through delivering sessions raising confidence in young people or through projects that help the community.

Georgia made contact with her careers advisory service (CAS) during her second year. University policy is to allocate careers consultants to subject departments and organise termly meetings with students. 'We learned about what the CAS could offer us and had sessions on what our career options were, how we could help our future careers by acquiring transferable skills, learned to use the CAS facilities, how to prepare applications, and could have individual consultations in our third year.'

Georgia used web-based information sites in the CAS offices, gained a lot of information from information assistants – and in the summer of her second year, with their help, found a paid internship with the NHS in Leeds. She also attended careers fairs held on campus.

In her final year a careers consultant helped her focus on what she wanted to do, gave her advice on writing a CV and preparing for interviews. She also had a mock interview with very good feedback and advice. 'This was amazingly helpful.'

What skills does Georgia think she gained from her time as a student?

'On my course I gained skills in numeracy, communication and working in a team. For my final year project for example, I had to work with seven people I did not know very well. We had to learn to work together quickly and share the work. I also prepared a personal employability plan – through sessions in my department led by CAS.'

Her university offers the York Award, a formal award which informs employers which activities students have been involved in and which skills they have gained. As one activity, Georgia followed a course in counselling, then worked as a mentor with a vulnerable adult in the local community, teaching her to use bus services and accompanying her to local clubs.

'Through my department, the CAS and the York Award, I gained in confidence, learned to believe in myself and realised that I could achieve what I wanted.'

Conclusion

It's helpful to have a career path in mind, even if it might change later as you progress through your course and gain experience. The earlier you start your research, the better your chance of making an informed decision – with the added benefit that evidence of your long-term approach will strengthen your UCAS application and improve your interview performance.

Resources

Publications

- *Choosing Your Degree Course & University*, Trotman Education, www.trotman.co.uk.
- *Getting into* series, Trotman Education, www.trotman.co.uk. Gives advice on securing a place at university for courses leading to professional careers (such as medicine, law, psychology, physiotherapy, engineering, pharmacy, veterinary school, and business and management courses), and on gaining places on courses at Oxford and Cambridge.
- *How to Write a Winning UCAS Personal Statement*, Trotman Education, www.trotman.co.uk.
- *If Only I'd Known, making the most of higher education, a guide for students and parents,* Association of Graduate Recruiters, www.qualityresearchinternational.com. Contains tips on making the most of higher education and how to gain the skills that will increase your employability.

- *STEM Careers*, Trotman Education, www.trotman.co.uk.
- *What Do Graduates Do?*, HECSU (Higher Education Careers Services Unit) and Association of Graduate Careers Advisory Services (AGCAS), www.hecsu.ac.uk.
- *You're Hired! CV*, Trotman, www.trotman.co.uk.
- *You're Hired! Graduate Career Handbook*, Trotman, www.trotman.co.uk.

IT programs

- Careerscape: information on careers and higher education courses, together with case studies and articles. This may be available in your school or college, at your local careers service or library (CAS-CAiD, www.cascaid.co.uk).
- Centigrade: assesses your academic and personal strengths (Cambridge Occupational Analysts, www.coa.co.uk). If it is not available at school or college you can access it yourself at Centigrade: www.coa.co.uk/programmes-and-aptitude-tests/centigrade.
- Morrisby Careers Questionnaire: assesses personal strengths and abilities. It is often used by careers teachers and advisers in schools or colleges. It may also be taken by individuals at home or at a centre. Details at www.morrisby.com.

The following resources may be available at your school, college, careers centre or library.

- Job Explorer Database (Jed): interactive, multimedia careers information resource in which students can explore 847 jobs in depth (2,300 individual career titles), with pictures and case studies of people at work. The section 'Higher ideas' shows which higher education courses connect with interests and subject choices (Careersoft, www.careersoft.co.uk).
- eCLIPS: allows users to search for careers against criteria such as work skills or school subjects, and also has a linked interest guide (www.eclips-online.co.uk). It contains information on over 1,200 jobs and careers.

Websites

- www.agcas.org.uk: Association of Graduate Careers Advisory Services.
- https://nationalcareersservice.direct.gov.uk. Search under 'job profiles'. The site contains over 800 listings.
- www.prospects.ac.uk: useful detailed information on graduate careers.
- www.do-it.org.uk: a national database of volunteering opportunities, listed by postcode area.

3 | A matter of money

If you have got this far in the book, you are serious about putting in a higher education application. Even before considering whether you are likely to achieve the entry grades for the course, you will probably have asked yourself, 'Can I afford it?'

Certainly, you will need to think through your finances very carefully and research all the types of assistance that will be available to you. There is a lot of information available – on government websites, on the UCAS website, from universities and colleges themselves and in books written specifically on this subject. A summary is given in this chapter, with details of where to look for more information in the 'Resources' section at the end.

In order to help you in your overall consideration of whether higher education is right for you, this chapter will look at the two main costs in attending higher education: tuition fees and living expenses.

All figures given in this chapter were current in February 2018. You can expect increases in further years and you will need to check for up-to-date rates.

Tuition fees

The cost of providing college and university courses is met partly by the government and partly through variable (top-up) tuition fees, which are the student's contribution.

The maximum annual tuition fees for students in England, Northern Ireland and Wales at many universities are £9,250. Universities and colleges decide for themselves how much to charge. They may all charge up to £6,000. If they wish to charge higher fees up to £9,000 they must prove that they will be awarding bursaries to poorer students by means of an access statement.

In addition, universities and colleges that meet a certain standard of teaching (as rated by the government through its new Teaching Excellence Framework) will be permitted to charge a higher figure. This is currently £9,250 and will almost certainly rise with inflation in later years.

According to the Government's Office for Fair Access (OFFA), 135 universities and colleges plan to charge the full £9,250 for at least one of their courses and 26 plan to do so for all their courses. (Source: *2018–19 access agreements and institutional expenditure and fee levels*. OFFA.)

There is no national list of fees charged – you will have to check individual websites.

You will not have to pay these fees in advance, however, unless you are able and willing to do so. You may take out a tuition fee loan; this is not means-tested and will not have to be repaid until after graduation when you are in employment and your earnings have exceeded £21,000 for students in England and Wales, and £17,495 for students in Scotland and Northern Ireland. These amounts are standard, but there are variations in how the rules are applied by individual nations within the UK.

The situation for students resident in one part of the UK but studying in another is complicated. Northern Irish, Scottish and Welsh universities will charge non-resident students higher tuition fees than those charged to their own residents. A summary of the information known at the time of writing (April 2017) follows. However, please check national websites for more recent information.

- In England, tuition fees are up to £9,250.
- In Northern Ireland, residents who study in Northern Ireland pay up to £4,030. Fees for other UK students attending university in Northern Ireland are not capped and could be up to £9,250.
- In Wales, tuition fees are up to £9,250 a year, but students who live in Wales pay only the first £4,296 and may apply for a means-tested grant from the Welsh Government of up to £4,954 to cover the remaining sum.
- In Scotland, Scottish students studying at Scottish universities **pay no fees.** If however, they study elsewhere in the UK they must pay up to £9,250.
- Students from England, Wales and Northern Ireland studying in Scotland must pay the full fees charged by individual universities and colleges. (Note that degree courses in Scotland are typically four years in length.)

You will see from the above that English students get a bad deal.

Living expenses

Living expenses include the cost of your accommodation, food, clothes, travel, books and equipment (plus possible extras such as field trips and study visits, if these are not covered by the tuition fees), as well as leisure and social activities.

It is impossible to suggest a standard amount for living expenses since they vary in different universities and colleges. Also, individual students' tastes, needs and priorities vary widely. Costs also vary according to the type of accommodation you choose. This is the factor that will most affect your expenditure. Some accommodation is luxury standard with on-site launderette, cinema, gym, games rooms and bars. Expect to pay accordingly! Not every option below is available at every university or college, but you might be able to choose between:

- a study bedroom in a hall of residence with an en suite bathroom
- a standard room, usually fitted with a hand basin, and shared baths/showers and lavatories
- a shared room (available in a minority of places); there can be as much as £3,000 per year difference between the cost of an en suite bedroom and a shared room
- meals provided – in halls, usually dinner and breakfast but some also provide lunch
- self-catering accommodation – i.e. with a shared kitchen with fridge, cooker, cupboards, etc. where you can prepare your own meals
- a room rented from a private landlord, often in a house or apartment shared with other students.

Many first-year students opt for the greater degree of privacy given by an en suite bathroom but from the second year onwards choose to share private houses with friends they made during their first year. Bathrooms are then shared as are kitchens and cooking facilities.

The information below gives you some idea of possible expenses.

- Try individual universities' and colleges' websites. Some are better than others and give breakdowns under various headings such as accommodation, food and daily travel. Others go further and give typical weekly, monthly or annual spends. They don't give this information in a standard format, however. Some give weekly figures; some monthly; others for an academic or calendar year. You need to be able to compare like with like. Are you interested in figures for term time only, term time plus Easter and Christmas vacations (particularly if you are an international student and not likely to go home then), or for a whole year if you think you might stay in your university or college town for twelve months?
- When considering accommodation it is also important to check such things as:
  - Will personal property insurance be included in accommodation fees?
  - Is there free wifi in the bedrooms?
  - Will a television licence also be included or will you have to pay for your own?
  - If you do not want to pay for an entire year's accommodation will you have to pay a small fee to keep your room reserved for you during Christmas and Easter vacations?
  - If you choose self-catering accommodation how many students share a kitchen?
- A quick snapshot of accommodation shows:
  - A university in the south of England had room rents varying from £5,886 for a single en suite room to £3,346 for a standard room.

- o A university in the north-west of England charged £5,651 for a single en suite room and up to £6,882 for a 'premier studio'. These are self-catering prices, but for an additional £40 per week students could have all meals – with packed lunches provided on request.
- o A Midlands university offered single en suite rooms from £5,811 and standard rooms from £4,485.
- o A university on the south coast of England offered en suite rooms at up to £6,500 and standard rooms from £4,200.
- o A Scottish university suggested an average cost of £1,100 per month, to include accommodation, food, energy bills, internet access and laundry bills.
- o In London individual universities charged from £5,256 for a standard room and from £5,300 to over £7,500 for an en suite room.

- You will probably be surprised when you do some research to find that the cheapest and most expensive towns are not as you might have expected. Much depends on how much accommodation is available and how much daily travel costs come to.
- The NUS (www.nus.org.uk) gives average costs for a 39-week academic year in towns throughout the UK, but its survey refers to England only.

TIPS!

Many universities have accommodation brochures which you can download.

In some towns a large amount of student accommodation is owned by private companies as opposed to the universities and colleges themselves. This option means you would share accommodation with students from other universities and colleges.

Funding your studies

How do you intend to fund your time in higher education? Don't ignore this question and leave it until the last minute! You will need to think carefully about how to budget for several years' costs – and you need to know what help you might be able to expect from:

- the government
- your parents or partner
- other sources.

One survey showed that on average 50% of students' income came from tuition fee and maintenance loans, 15% from paid work and varying amounts (depending on family income) from non-repayable grants and bursaries, and other sources such as families and scholarships.

This chapter gives a brief overview of a complicated funding situation, which varies according to where you come from and where you plan to study. For more details about all the different types of funding available and how to apply for them, please consult your own national website.

Tuition fee loans

These are available in England, Northern Ireland and Wales. If you take one out (and most students do), the Student Loans Company will pay your fees directly to your university or college at the start of each year of your course, adding the interest to your repayable loan total. The loan will be repaid through the income tax system. That means that once you are working, your employer will take the required amount from your salary and make the payments – 9% of your income above £21,000 (£17,495 for students in Northern Ireland). Payments increase when graduates earn above £41,000. (If you had started repaying the loan, then lost your job or had a pay cut, then your repayments would drop accordingly.)

- The current situation regarding repayments means that you will repay 9% of anything you earn above £21,000 (£17,495 for students in Northern Ireland) each year, starting after you graduate – or leave your course early. The interest rate is changed each September, and is normally based on the previous March's RPI (Retail Prices Index) rate of inflation plus 3%. In February 2018 the interest rate was 6.1%. However, by the time you read this, this figure might have changed if the bank base rate has increased or decreased. (The Retail Prices Index is a measure of UK inflation; it measures changes to the cost of living in the UK.)
- If you have not cleared your debt 30 years after graduation, it will be cancelled.

Maintenance or living costs loans

In addition to a tuition fee loan, all students may apply for a maintenance or living cost loan. The maximum amount available per year is £11,354, which is based on what a student from England might receive if studying in London. Figures for students from Wales, Scotland and Northern Ireland will vary slightly. All students are entitled to a maintenance loan; however, part of this amount will be dependent on your household income – in other words, it is means-tested. 'Household income' refers to your family's gross annual income (their income before tax) of the household you live in. Certain pensions contributions and allowances for dependent children are also deducted from the figure to achieve the total sum.

The maximum annual loan in England (2018–19):

- £7,324 for those living in the family home
- £8,700 for those studying away from home (£11,354 in London)
- £9,963 for students spending a year of a UK course overseas.

In Northern Ireland (2017–18):

- £3,750 for those living in the family home
- £4,840 for those studying away from home (£6,780 in London)
- £5,770 for students spending a year of a UK course overseas.

In Wales (2018–19):

- £6,650 for those living in the family home
- £8,000 for those studying away from home (£10,250 in London)
- £8,000 for students spending a year of a UK course overseas.

In Scotland (2017–18):

- £5,750.

(Later figures for Northern Ireland and Scotland were not available at the time of writing.)

Maintenance loans are repaid in the same way as loans for tuition fees. Extra help may be available for students with disabilities and for those on low incomes or who have dependants.

Additional support

Bursaries and scholarships

What is the difference? Bursaries are usually non-competitive and automatic, often based on financial need, while scholarships are competitive and you usually have to apply for them. However, many universities and colleges use the terms interchangeably.

In addition to the funding described above, most universities and colleges offer tuition fee bursaries, mainly to students who receive the maximum maintenance loan. These bursaries cover part or all of the cost of the course and are awarded according to the universities' own criteria, but they are often worked out according to the level of parental income. Approximately one-third of students receive some kind of financial assistance in this way.

Some universities and colleges offer scholarships to students enrolling on certain courses *or* to students with the highest entry grades. Merit-based scholarships and prizes are also sometimes available once you have started university, for example, if you have performed particularly well in end-of-year examinations.

Students leaving care

Care leavers receive a one-off bursary of £2,000 which their local education authorities are obliged to pay – and may also apply for additional funds. Many universities and colleges offer further support and are often able to provide accommodation for the whole year – which means that students do not have to move out during vacations. Check out the information specially written for care leavers on the UCAS website.

Other help from universities and colleges

Not all help comes in the form of cash. Students may receive any of the following – again probably dependent on income:

- assistance with cost of compulsory field trips and visits
- help to purchase laboratory clothing
- free laptops.

Additional financial support may be available to students with disabilities, for those with dependants and for mature students with existing financial commitments. These regulations are subject to change so it is essential to check them.

Other bursaries and scholarships

Students on particular courses, with particular career aspirations or with particular personal circumstances may be eligible for extra financial help. It is worth consulting the sources listed at the end of this chapter to find out whether you might be eligible for a grant made by a particular professional organisation or charity.

Sponsorship

Students applying for particular courses – for example accountancy, business studies and engineering – can sometimes be sponsored by employers or related organisations. In return for a sum of money paid to you as a student you would normally be expected to work for your sponsor during some of your vacations. Naturally, if you were suitable they would expect you to work for them for a period after you graduated. (However, the number of sponsorships available to new students has declined. Many employers now prefer to sponsor students whom they select during the first or second year of their courses.)

Degree apprenticeships

Students don't pay for training or tuition fees – these are covered by the employer and the government. You will be paid a wage throughout the course for your employment, which will help to cover your living costs. Degree apprentices are not entitled to student loans.

NHS Bursaries

Students on degree courses in medicine and dentistry are treated in the same way as students on other degree programmes for the first four years of their courses. However, NHS funding to assist with or cover tuition and living expenses is available to these students from the fifth year. These bursaries are income-related. The system is not the same in all countries in the UK, so you must check your national student finance websites.

> **TIP!**
>
> Make a note of any deadlines for loan or funding applications and ensure that you have completed all of the necessary paperwork.

Other sources of cash

Part-time work

For many students, there will be a continual need to balance studies with part-time employment. One report showed that the annual average amount earned was £3,500. This is something to think about when you make your selection of universities and colleges. Some towns have many more opportunities than others. In an area of high unemployment, for instance, all the jobs may be taken by permanent workers. In more affluent areas there might be more hourly paid work available – especially at hours when students are willing to work. You can check out the local employment situation on universities' and colleges' websites.

Here are some additional ideas to bear in mind.

- Many universities and colleges help by running their own jobs banks. Students can get work, for example, in the students' union, libraries or offices (secretarial and administrative work if they have the skills), or in catering, domestic or manual work.
- Other opportunities often include guiding visitors around the campus or acting as student guides on open days.
- Most universities and colleges also have a job shop provided by student services or the careers advisory service that advertises jobs in the town or city.
- A useful website with a number of part-time jobs is www.fish4.co.uk.

However, many higher education courses include practical coursework, field studies and/or time spent abroad, which leave little opportunity for employment except during vacations. Additionally, it is often recommended that students spend no more than 15 hours a week in paid employment if their studies are not to suffer. Oxford and Cambridge do not encourage any of their students to work during their (particularly short) term times.

If you are an international student, you will need to check the wording on your visa regarding part-time work. It may say that you are permitted to work for a certain number of hours – or, that you may not do any paid employment at all.

> **TIP!**
>
> Check the cost of living and employment availability in the towns where you might be going to live during term time. This will help you estimate what your living costs are likely to be and your chances of finding part-time work.

Banking deals

Many students take advantage of the student banking deals available from a number of high street banks. These can include interest-free overdrafts (which are advisable as a last resort only because they do have to be repaid – and interest rates on late payments can be very high) as well as various other freebies such as free driving lessons or railcards. You should shop around carefully for the deal that best suits your priorities – and remember, the advice that banks give on their websites is unlikely to be wholly impartial.

> **TIP!**
>
> Try not to run up a large overdraft or credit card debts, as in the long run you can end up paying large sums of interest on the money owed.

Many universities and colleges have student financial advisers whom students can approach for help. A students' union is also a good source of information and advice on financial assistance.

Students from the European Union

Students from the European Union have until now paid the same tuition fees as UK students and were eligible to apply for a tuition fees loan (or free tuition in Scotland).

Following the Brexit referendum, students who applied for courses in 2018–19 were guaranteed that funding arrangements would remain the same for the duration of the course under the current terms.

The situation for future years is not yet known and is to be negotiated as part of the UK's formal discussions with the other Member States following Britain's exit from the EU. Therefore, for the time being, until it is announced otherwise, EU students will continue to pay the same fees as Home students.

International students

There is no control over fees that can be charged to international students – so you must shop around and consult individual university and college websites. Courses are often assigned to a *band* and fees charged accordingly.

For **Band A** courses, the clinical years of medicine and dentistry, typical fees in 2018–2019 were £42,000

Band B laboratory-based courses: £16,000–£21,000

Band C business studies and social sciences: £14,050–£16,620

Band D humanities: £13,000–£16,650.

Conclusion

Money can be a major headache for students, so it is well worth taking the time to work out how you're going to fund yourself. It's also very important to be on top of all the paperwork required for loan applications because missed deadlines can mean that you start your course before your loan comes through.

> **TIP!**
>
> All students are advised to apply to the appropriate authority for funding as soon as they have firmly accepted an offer of a place.

Resources

Publications

- Various Child Poverty Action Group titles, most of which are also available online, for example *Welfare Benefits and Tax Credits*

Handbook, Student Support and Benefits Handbook, Council Tax Handbook and *Child Support Handbook*, for England, Wales and Northern Ireland. Available at www.cpag.org.uk.
- For Scottish residents, as above plus *Benefits for Students in Scotland Handbook*, available from Child Poverty Action Group in Scotland at www.cpag.org.uk/scotland.

Official organisations

- www.gov.uk/education/student-grants-bursaries-scholarships.
- www.gov.uk/student-finance-calculator (helps you to estimate which loans and other sources of funding you might be able to get).
- www.gov.uk/contact-student-finance-england.
- www.studentfinanceni.co.uk.
- www.studentfinancewales.co.uk.
- www.saas.gov.uk.
- www.gov.uk/extra-money-pay-university (for information on bursaries and scholarships).

General student support

- www.thescholarshiphub.org.uk: information on possible bursaries, scholarships, sponsors and degree apprenticeships.
- www.moneysavingexpert.com/students: site of money expert Martin Lewis, which gives helpful advice on all aspects of student budgeting.
- www.nhsbsa.nhs.uk/816.aspx: information on NHS student bursaries.
- www.nus.org.uk: the National Union of Students.
- www.ucas.com/ucas/undergraduate/undergraduate-finance-and-support. (You can also contact UCAS through Facebook and Twitter.)
- www.slc.co.uk: the Student Loans Company.
- www.propel.org.uk: a specialist website for prospective students leaving care.
- www.becomecharity.org.uk (formerly the Who Cares Trust) for young care leavers.

Part-time and temporary jobs

- www.student-jobs.co.uk.
- www.e4s.co.uk.
- www.fish4.co.uk.

4| Choosing what to study

You are probably already aware that there is a vast number of subjects on offer. You can get an idea of the full range by exploring the UCAS search tool at www.ucas.com and the other resources listed on page 44.

You may enter up to five course choices on your UCAS application. However, if you are applying for medicine, dentistry or veterinary science you are limited to four courses in your chosen subject, although you can make one additional application to a course in another subject – see Chapter 8 for more information.

So how do you start to narrow it down? This chapter covers some of the questions you should be asking yourself so that you can focus your research on the courses that will be best suited to your interests.

Which subject area?

If you have got this far, it is likely that you have some idea of what subject area you would like to pursue further. If not, here are a few questions to think about.

- Which of the subjects you are currently studying interests you most? Are you interested enough to want to study it for the next few years?
- Are you interested in one particular aspect of your advanced-level course? If so, you may find that specialist higher education courses will allow you to focus on this particular aspect.
- What are your career plans? What are the entry requirements for that career? Which courses match this best?
- Are you prepared to undergo more specific job-related training as a postgraduate? If not, should you be looking for a vocational (career related) course that leads directly into an occupation?

There are two useful ICT programs that can help you to choose a course. They might be available for you to use at your school, college or local careers centre.

Higher Ideas

Using this program you can find out which higher education courses tie in with your interests and school subject choices, and from there:

- course content
- which universities and colleges offer them
- what qualifications you might need
- how to find out more.

You can do all of this searching different UK regions.

Information is held on over 41,000 courses.

This program has a link to the Job Explorer Database referred to in Chapter 2.

Centigrade

You can use this program to indicate courses that might appeal to you by completing an online questionnaire which is used to assess your interests, abilities and personal qualities. This assessment matches your replies with courses of higher education at mainly degree, HND or Diploma levels. The program searches:

- the current UCAS database of courses and universities
- a CAO (Central Applications Office, Ireland) database of courses and universities in Ireland
- a database of all courses in European higher education institutions taught in English
- a database of all courses in Canada taught in English
- a database of all courses in Australia and New Zealand
- any ideas of courses you might already have.

You will receive a list of courses to investigate and an action plan suggesting further research. If it is not available at school or college you can access it yourself at www.centigradeonline.co.uk. The cost is £15.

The 'Resources' section at the end of Chapter 2 should give you some more ideas of where to start your research.

Which qualification?

It is important to know something about each of the different types of qualification on offer so that you can select the one that is most suitable for you.

For example, course lengths (and therefore expenses) vary widely. A list of the main options is given below, and each course type is explored in more depth in the paragraphs that follow.

- DipHEs.
- HNDs.
- Foundation degrees.
- Ordinary first degrees: the lowest grade of degree awarded.
- Honours first degrees: divided into four classes (first, upper second, lower second and third).
- Courses leading to the award of a master's degree.

See the 'Degree courses' section below for further explanation of first (or bachelor's) degrees and master's degrees.

DipHEs

Some universities and colleges offer undergraduate courses leading to a DipHE (Diploma of Higher Education). Two-year full-time DipHE courses are normally equivalent to the first two years of a degree and can often be used for entry to the final year of a related degree course. They are mainly linked to performance or vocational areas such as animal studies, dance education, health and social care, and paramedic practice, although some universities and colleges offer them in humanities subjects, including English and history.

HNDs

A Higher National Diploma (HND) is a vocational qualification which is roughly equivalent to the first two years of a three-year degree course.

Many universities and colleges offer HND courses in the same subject areas as their degree courses, giving students the option to transfer between courses or to top up their HND to a degree through a further year's study. In fact the majority of students do so, either by taking a special one-year top-up course or by transferring to the second or third year of a degree course in a similar subject at their university or college. Keep this in mind when planning your application strategy. With a few exceptions such as art and design, health and social care, performing arts and hospitality management, HNDs fall into two main subject areas: science, construction, engineering and technology, and business studies and related subjects.

Science, construction, engineering and technology

Courses at all levels in these categories attract comparatively fewer applications than business and finance courses. It is therefore likely that if you apply for a degree in, for example, mechanical engineering at an institution that also offers an HND in engineering, admissions tutors will make you an offer covering both the degree and the HND course, but with different conditions for each (normally lower for the HND).

Business studies and related subjects

For HND courses in this subject area, the picture is rather different. HND courses usually attract a large number of applications in their own right: many students deliberately opt for the HND courses because they are shorter and often more specialised than the degrees. It is therefore less usual for universities and colleges to make dual offers for degrees and HNDs. This means that you must consider your options very carefully.

If you have doubts about your ability to reach the level required for degree entry, you may be best advised to apply for the HND. You must talk through the options with your teachers or careers adviser before making these difficult decisions.

Foundation degrees

As with HNDs, these courses focus on a particular job or profession. They are mainly offered in colleges of further or higher education in partnership with universities but also in some universities, and are available in England, Northern Ireland and Wales. Full-time courses last two years and, like HNDs (which in some subject areas foundation degrees have replaced), can be converted into honours degrees with a subsequent year of full-time study. Designed by business and industry to meet their skills needs, foundation degrees were originally developed to train employees in particular career sectors as higher technicians or associate professionals, but entry to full-time courses is now available to anyone.

Foundation degrees combine academic study with the development of work-related skills. Programmes are offered in areas such as digital media arts, business and management, horticulture, equine studies, hospitality, fashion design and a vast range of other subjects. Foundation degree courses lead to the awards of:

- FdA (arts)
- FdEng (engineering)
- FdSci (science).

There are no set entry requirements for foundation degrees. Formal qualifications are not always necessary since commercial and industrial experience can be more relevant. All foundation degrees take into account work experience. Entry requirements can therefore be very flexible.

Degree courses

Bachelor's degrees

In England, Northern Ireland and Wales, first degree courses usually last three years (sometimes four, if a year abroad or in industry is included) and lead to the award of a bachelor's degree. The title of the degree awarded usually reflects the subject studied.

Some of the more common ones are:

- BA: Bachelor of Arts
- BCom: Bachelor of Commerce
- BEng: Bachelor of Engineering
- BMus: Bachelor of Music
- BSc: Bachelor of Science
- LLB: Bachelor of Law.

The exceptions to this are the universities of Oxford and Cambridge (Oxbridge), which award a BA regardless of the subject. (Oxbridge graduates are then able to upgrade to a master's degree, without further exams, about four years later.)

Master's degrees

In England, Northern Ireland and Wales, master's degrees are usually acquired via a completely different course that must be applied for separately and cannot be taken until the bachelor's degree has been completed.

However, some first degree courses lead directly to the award of a master's degree (e.g. MEd, MEng, MPhys and MSc). These courses are usually extended or enhanced versions of the bachelor's course, last at least four years, and are likely to be in engineering or science disciplines.

Scottish universities and colleges

At Scottish universities and colleges standard bachelor's degrees normally last for four years rather than three, and students typically take a broad range of subjects in the first two years before going on to specialise in the final two years. At some universities and colleges students are awarded a master's as standard for a four-year degree in arts, humanities and social science subjects, while science students receive a BSc. Most students in Scotland enter higher education aged 18 after six years of secondary education, although a significant minority will enter after only five years and therefore be 17 when they start university.

Single, joint or combined honours?

Most universities and colleges offer single, joint and combined honours degree courses. Combined honours courses enable you to combine several areas of interest and may lead you to an interesting programme or additional career opportunities (for example, studying biology with French may enable you to work in France).

It is important to check the weighting given to each subject in a combined course. Popular ones include 50/50 and 75/25. As a general rule you can assume that *Subject A AND Subject B* means equal time given to each whereas *Subject A WITH Subject B* means much less time spent on the second or minor subject. BUT this is not always so. Universities and colleges are able to decide on their own course titles. The only way to be sure that you know what you are getting is to study course information very carefully.

If you intend to take a joint or combined honours course, do be aware that you will be kept busier than you would be on a single honours course. It can be a struggle if you have to make your own connections between the modules of study, and the work may not be well coordinated. Ask individual departments' admissions tutors as soon as possible about the possibilities and potential problems of combining courses.

Degree classification

Honours degrees are classified as:

- First Class
- Upper Second Class (2.i)
- Lower Second Class (2.ii)
- Third Class.

Ordinary and pass degrees are awarded, depending on the system, to those not pursuing honours courses or to narrow failures on honours courses.

Which mode of study?

While full-time study is the most popular choice, there are also the following options.

Part-time

Part-time study is becoming more popular as students increasingly find it necessary to work in order to finance their studies; on the other hand, it can be difficult to balance the demands of a job and higher education, so you should make sure you do some thorough research before making your decision.

Distance learning

This option was once available only through the Open University but is now offered by many universities and colleges. It is ideal for people who want to work in a full-time job and study in their spare time. They receive on-line course material and support and usually attend weekend courses or summer schools. This route obviously requires a lot of commitment.

Sandwich courses

Many degrees and HNDs offer periods of work experience from three to 12 months. The 12-month programmes add a year to your course.

Study abroad

Many universities and colleges have links with partner organisations. In addition you may be able to participate in the Erasmus Programme. The programme is named after Erasmus of Rotterdam, the Dutch philosopher who lived and worked in several countries, but is also an acronym, meaning **EuR**opean Community **A**ction **S**cheme for the **M**obility of **U**niversity **S**tudents. Students who join the Erasmus Programme study for at least three months or do an internship for a period of at least two months to an academic year at one of more than 4,000 higher education institutions in another European country. They do not pay extra tuition fees to the university that they visit and can apply for an Erasmus grant to help cover the additional expense of living abroad. It is not yet known whether the UK will continue to participate in the programme after Brexit, although two other non-EU members – Iceland and Norway – do.

Sponsored study

Sponsorship is sometimes offered to students on certain courses. In some cases students apply for a degree or HND course through UCAS and the university or college helps to arrange their training placement. (Full sponsorship is becoming rarer however, since, increasingly, employers are offering sponsorship only from the second year of a course. It's important, therefore, to check which ones have links with particular universities and colleges.)

If a sponsor requires you to attend a particular university or college, the sponsor will inform you and the institution will sort out the UCAS arrangements.

Degree apprenticeships

Degree apprenticeships are organised differently from sponsorship programmes.

They offer the opportunity to gain a full bachelor's degree through an arrangement between employers and higher education institutions. Part-time study takes place at a university or college, with the rest of your time being with your employer. They can take from three to six years to complete, depending on the course level. Currently, the scheme is only available in England and Wales, although applications may be made from all parts of the UK.

Degree apprenticeships are still quite new, so there is currently a limited number of vacancies, most of which are in the business and finance areas.

Which courses?

This is, of course, the million-dollar question! Having thought about the above points, you should now have a clearer idea of the type of qualification and subject area for which you would like to apply. However, there may still be hundreds of courses on offer fitting the criteria you have determined so far – so this is the point where you really must start to narrow down your options. The only way to do this is by thorough research, which means looking through directories, prospectuses and websites and visiting specific departments at specific universities.

Here are some of the things you should take into account.

- **Course content**: there can be a whole world of difference between courses with exactly the same title, so take a detailed look at the content and see how it relates to your particular interests. How much do you want to specialise? How much freedom do you want in selecting your options?
- **Teaching and assessment methods**: again, these can vary widely. For example, some courses may be very practical, with workshops and case studies, while others may be centred on essays and tutorials. If you do not perform well in exams, you can search for courses assessed via modules and projects.
- **Professional accreditation**: if you are planning to enter a specific career for which professional accreditation is required (for example law, engineering or accountancy), it is well worth checking out which courses offer full or partial exemption from the exams required to gain this accreditation.
- **Links with industry**: some courses and departments have strong links with industry, which can help graduates secure jobs.
- **Graduate destinations**: these are often listed on universities' and colleges' websites and can help you assess whether the course will give you the skills you will need in the workplace.

> **TIP!**
>
> Use the UCAS search tool, which enables you to search courses by a wide range of features including subject, region and town. There is also the ability to filter searches by qualification level, study mode, and single or combined subjects. You will also find entry requirements and tuition fees for courses and access to university and college websites.

Conclusion

You should now be able to begin to develop a clear idea of the kind of course you would like to apply for. However, two aspects of the decision-making process have yet to be discussed: your choice of university or college and entry requirements. These factors are examined in detail in the following chapters.

Resources

Publications

- *Choosing Your Degree Course & University*, Trotman Education, www.trotman.co.uk.
- *Heap 2019: University Degree Course Offers*, Trotman Education, www.trotman.co.uk.
- *The University Choice Journal*, Trotman, www.trotman.co.uk.
- *What Do Graduates Do?*, HECSU and AGCAS, www.hecsu.ac.uk.

IT programs

- Higher Ideas: www.careersoft.co.uk/Products/Higher_Ideas.
- Centigrade:www.coa.co.uk/programmes-and-aptitude-tests/centigrade.
- ERASMUS:www.erasmusplus.org.uk.

Websites

- www.ucas.com: begin with 'Getting started'. (You can also contact UCAS through Facebook and Twitter.)
- www.push.co.uk.
- www.theguardian.com/education/universityguide.
- www.timeshighereducation.com.
- www.telegraph.co.uk/education/universities-colleges.

Higher education exhibitions

UCAS organises a network of over 50 exhibitions, held at exhibition centres in different regions. If you can manage to go to one you will find universities, colleges, gap year organisations and some employers all under one roof. You will be able to ask individual questions as well as attend presentations on topics such as applications, finance and accommodation. At many exhibitions there are separate presentations on finance for parents.

In addition to general exhibitions there is a specialist one, 'Create your Future', which takes place in London and Manchester, for students interested in studying a creative, media or performance-related subject.

You can find out more information at www.ucas.com/exhibitions.

Taster courses

Many universities and colleges hold these during the summer holidays. If you can manage to attend one you will get an insight into what life as a student will be like. Courses last from one day to one week and typically include the opportunity to attend lectures and classes as well as sampling the accommodation and seeing the campus.

5 | Choosing where to study

The previous chapter should have helped you build up a picture of your ideal course and start to create a shortlist. However, it's still likely that a lot more than five courses will fit the bill, so you need to narrow the list down further.

Now is the time to start thinking about which university or college you would like to study at.

Working out your priorities

There are 395 institutions in the UCAS scheme that offer higher education courses, including universities, colleges of higher education and further education colleges. Very different considerations and priorities affect each person's choice of institution. To give you some idea of the range, current students say they were influenced by one or more of the following factors.

Academic factors

- The type of course you are looking for.
- The reputation for research in a particular department.
- Quality of teaching. You can find out more about this by consulting the Teaching Excellence and Student Outcomes Framework document at http://www.hefce.ac.uk/lt/tef.
- The status of the university/college as a whole. If you feel concerned about this point, you can consult various league tables. The reliability of these varies, however: the *Guardian*, *The Times* and *The Complete University Guide* are more impartial sources. You could also seek advice from professional bodies and/or employers.
- Entry requirements: be honest with yourself about your potential results at advanced level. It is better to face reality now than to be forced to revise your plans several months later.
- Number of student places on particular courses: the bigger the intake target, usually the better your chances. Prospectuses and websites give an indication of the size of intake, but remember that

their numbers may include students on both single and combined or modular degrees.

- Employability of graduates.

Social factors

- Location: do you like the big city or countryside? Do you want to be on a campus or in the middle of a city? Are you trying to stay within easy reach of home, or get as far away as possible?
- Popularity of the university/college.
- Facilities for sport, leisure activities, music, etc.
- Cost of living.
- Accommodation: is there enough of it? Does it suit your preferences, e.g. self-catering or with meals provided?
- Financial support offered to students (e.g. bursaries and scholarships).
- Level of support and facilities for students with disabilities.

The list of factors you might want to consider could go on forever. You will have to draw the line somewhere and then work out which are most important to you personally.

Once you have decided on your key priorities, where do you start to find out the answers to all your questions? The 'Resources' section at the end of this chapter lists publications and websites that collate this type of information. Using these as a first port of call can speed up your research no end, but there is no substitute for first-hand research through, for example, university/college open days, websites and prospectuses.

It is also well worth talking to former students from your school or college, family friends and older brothers and sisters about their experiences. More advice on this is given in the 'Researching your shortlist' section below.

TIP!

Don't forget to get university prospectuses (download or request a hard copy) and look at university/college websites.

Staying close to home?

A growing number of students apply only to universities and colleges that are within daily commuting distance, opting to save on living expenses while enjoying the support and comforts of home. With current tuition fees of up to £9,250 (depending on which country in the

UK you live in and where in the UK you choose to study), the choice of living in a hall of residence or in rented accommodation may be an option for fewer and fewer students. But, don't forget, as mentioned in Chapter 3, in some towns where you might assume that living costs are high, rents can be lower than you think and it can be very easy to find part-time jobs.

Studying from home can limit your 'student experience', as time spent travelling cuts down your opportunities for involvement in societies and social activities. You may also be less likely to network and make new friends, especially if you still have close friends from school living in the area. For parents and siblings, having a full-time student living at home can create tensions as time goes by.

You may decide on a compromise solution. A growing number of higher education courses – HNDs, foundation degrees, even first degree courses – start with a year studying at a local, franchised further education college before transferring to the parent campus to complete your degree.

Researching your shortlist

As soon as you feel ready, draw up your shortlist of about 10 possible courses from which you will select up to five (or four) final choices for your UCAS application. For each of your shortlist entries, make sure you have considered the following questions.

- What will I actually be studying on this course?
- Do I like the environment?
- Where is the course held? Many universities and colleges have several campuses. To avoid possible disappointment, research this now, as you wouldn't want to find yourself on a small satellite campus when you really wanted to be at the main site – or vice versa.
- Where will I live?
- Which options can I select on this course?
- How is progress assessed?
- Is there a tutorial system and how much support and advice on learning do students get?
- Can I achieve the qualifications needed for entry? (For help on this last point, see the next chapter.)

On the UCAS website you can find entries from individual universities and colleges. Most use the following format:

- Why study this course? Gives details on the topics studied and teaching and learning methods.
- Exchange possibilities with universities or colleges in other countries. Many institutions offer the opportunity to spend part of your

course in another country – in Europe or much further afield – in the USA, Canada or Hong Kong for example. The list is almost endless.

- Location.
- Who is this course for?
- More about this course: Description of individual modules, compulsory and optional. Equipment needed.
- Modular structure.
- Skills and experience gained.
- After the course: Information on careers entered by previous graduates.

> **TIP!**
>
> Keep the prospectuses of places to which you are definitely applying!

It is important to attend open days and taster sessions at universities and colleges that really appeal to you, and talk with student ambassadors, who will attempt to answer your questions on any subject. You can also write and arrange a visit to the department by yourself. Also make sure to spend some time in the town or city where the college or university is based; it is really important that you have some experience of a place where you may spend three or four years.

For students with disabilities, this is particularly important – you need to make sure, before you apply to a university or college, that it will be able to meet your particular needs. For example, some campuses are better than others for wheelchairs, while some have special facilities for people who are visually impaired or deaf. Get in touch with the disability officers at your shortlisted universities or colleges. More information about access and facilities for students with disabilities is also available at www.ucas.com/ucas/undergraduate/getting-started/individual-needs/disabled-students and, of course, from the prospectuses and websites of the universities and colleges themselves.

Parents can help with weighing up the issues and are excellent as sounding boards, but their advice and knowledge on today's degree courses, their applicability and relevance may well be out of date. (For example, some of the new UK universities have the best resourced and most reputable courses of applied study that feed into new careers in multimedia and technological industries – but, equally, some of the newer universities and colleges are under-resourced and have poor teaching reputations.)

You should also attend your nearest UCAS higher education exhibition to talk directly with representatives from higher education about courses. They are free to attend but you will need to book a place – either through school or college or individually.

Read the details concerning courses that interest you and for which you think realistically that you can match the entry requirements. Highlight important points you may want to address in the personal statement part of your UCAS application, or refer to at interview, several months ahead.

> **TIPS!**
>
> Do not take anything as given. Email or phone departments directly and ask to speak to the admissions tutor if you want to ask questions about the destinations of course graduates, possible career progression, admission details – anything. Tutors can be helpful and informative: they aren't there just to teach.
>
> If you cannot get to any open days try watching UCAS's online virtual tours of different universities and colleges.

Selecting the final five

If there is one particular university or college you want to attend (perhaps because you are a mature student and cannot move away from home), you can use your choices to apply for more than one course at the same institution. (Note that this is not possible at Oxford and Cambridge.) On the other hand, at some universities or colleges it is not necessary to apply for more than one course because admission is to a faculty or group of related subjects.

The other major factor to consider in selecting your final five courses is the entry requirements. Most universities and colleges supply entry requirements for their courses on the UCAS website. In order to maximise your chance of success, you need to make sure you apply to courses that are likely to make you an offer corresponding roughly with the grades you expect to achieve. This question is examined in greater detail in the next chapter.

Resources

Publications

- *Choosing Your Degree Course & University*, Trotman Education, www.trotman.co.uk.
- *Heap 2019: University Degree Course Offers,* Trotman Education, www.trotman.co.uk.
- *The University Choice Journal*, Trotman, www.trotman.co.uk.

Websites

General

- www.ucas.com: start with 'Getting started'. (You can also contact UCAS through Facebook and Twitter.)
- ucas.com/open-days.
- ucas.com/taster-courses.
- ucas.com/virtual-tours.
- www.push.co.uk.
- www.theguardian.com/education/universityguide.
- www.telegraph.co.uk/education/universities-colleges.
- www.thecompleteuniversityguide.co.uk.

For students with disabilities

- www.rnib.org.uk: Royal National Institute of Blind People.
- www.actiononhearingloss.org.uk: Action on Hearing Loss (formerly the Royal National Institute for Deaf People).
- www.disabilityrightsuk.org: Disability Rights UK (information for students with disabilities).

Case study

Sam, now in his first year at university, began to research universities in the first year of his A levels. Knowing that he wanted to be an engineer and hoping to work eventually in the Formula One industry, he chose to study mechanical engineering.

How did he make a shortlist of universities and how did he arrive at the final five?

'My first decision was that I didn't want to go a very long way from home. After that I consulted *The Complete University Guide* and used the league tables. My parents had read various articles in the *Daily Telegraph* and we compared notes. I also did a lot of research online through UCAS and university websites and student reviews.

'My sixth-form college was very helpful. In my first year they organised a university fair. Representatives from universities came to college to set up information stands. We could talk to as many as we wanted and they all issued invitations to open days if you were interested.

'I got my shortlist down to eight universities and in the summer holidays I went to open days at all but one of them. (I had decided before the date of the last one that I already had seven places I would be very happy with.) The open days all followed a similar

pattern, with general presentations on being a student, accommodation and finance, with tours and visits to individual departments.
We were able to ask any questions we had and also to talk to
students already doing mechanical engineering. My father drove
me to all the open days – and at all of them there were information
sessions specially for parents.'

6 | Academic requirements

You may have been thinking since Year 10 or 11 about whether you will be able to meet higher education entry requirements, planning how your A levels, Scottish Highers, IB, ILC or BTEC National Awards will build a foundation on which you will be able to progress into higher education. On the other hand, you may not have given the matter any serious thought yet.

Whatever the case, it is important to make sure you are realistic about the grades you hope to achieve and that you target your applications to suitable universities and colleges.

This chapter will help you understand how they set their entry requirements and offers some basic dos and don'ts relating to the final five courses you select.

What might the entry requirements be?

Would-be higher education entrants normally need to achieve minimum qualifications equivalent to one of the following:

- two A levels
- one Double Award A level
- the Cambridge Pre-U
- one BTEC National Award
- two Advanced Highers
- an ILC
- an IB.

See pages 58–62 for a full list.

You will also need supporting National 5s (Scotland only) at grades A–C or GCSEs at grades A*–C (Wales and Northern Ireland) or GCSEs at grades A*–C or 9–4/5 depending on requirements at different institutions (England). (Note that requirements vary for mature students and other groups – see page 81.)

In reality, however, most universities and colleges require more than the absolute minimum and many demand particular subjects for entry.

There are two main reasons for admission to some courses requiring higher than minimum grades.

1. **Coping with the course**: for the study of some subjects, a higher education department or faculty can decide that all its students need to achieve a particular qualification (say, B or C in A level Mathematics) in order to get through the course.
2. **Rationing places**: where there is high demand for a course the entry requirements will rise, because if a course asks for three Bs, fewer applicants will qualify for entry than if three Cs were requested (even though the three-C candidates might cope perfectly well with the course); grade requirements help to prevent courses from becoming oversubscribed.

The second of these two reasons is the more common – and it's therefore worth being aware that high grades are often an indication of popularity, and not always of quality. Some universities, colleges and courses are more popular than others and can therefore set high grades if they feel that the 'market' in a particular subject will bear them. It is worth knowing which courses are usually the most in demand.

On the closing date for applications, 15 January, in 2018 (for 2018 entry), the top ten subject groups chosen by applicants were:

1. subjects allied to medicine (down 9%)
2. business and administrative studies (down 4%)
3. biological sciences (up 1%)
4. creative arts and design (down 4%)
5. social studies (down 2%)
6. engineering (down 3%)
7. law (up 4%)
8. computer sciences (down 1%)
9. physical sciences (down 9%)
10. medicine and dentistry (up 9%).

In addition, any course with a special feature (such as sponsorship or an exchange with a university or college overseas) can attract large numbers of applications and may therefore also require high grades.

Whatever course you apply for, your qualifications are bound to be examined carefully by admissions tutors. They will be looking at your advanced-level study and checking that you are:

- offering the right subjects to satisfy entry requirements
- offering subjects they are prepared to include in an offer
- offering the types of qualification they want (e.g. A level, BTEC National)
- offering the right number of qualifications

- making an effort to fill any gaps in your record (e.g. by retaking GCSE mathematics at the same time as or before your advanced qualifications).

Admissions tutors will be on the lookout for students who are repeating advanced-level qualifications; your UCAS application must give full details of your results at the first attempt and include details of what you are repeating and when (see Chapter 15). Further explanations should be given in your personal statement.

Many admissions tutors will also attach a lot of importance to your results at GCSE or National 5 level. After all, these results, together with your predicted grades, will usually be the only evidence of your academic achievement to date. Tutors will be looking for:

- a reasonable spread of academic qualifications
- key subjects (e.g. English language and mathematics – as even if the university or college does not require them, most employers do)
- signs of academic capacity or potential.

Additional and alternative entry requirements

Applicants to music, art and design and other creative or performing arts courses often have to compile a portfolio of work, and may also have to attend an audition. (See Chapter 9 for more information.)

Should you wish to train for work with young children or vulnerable adults (for example in teaching, social work or the healthcare professions), the university or college will ask that you agree to have a criminal record check from one of the national disclosure and barring services, known as a DBS check (see Chapter 12).

Applicants for healthcare courses such as medicine, dentistry, nursing or midwifery may be asked for certificates to prove that they are not infected with any of the hepatitis viruses or tuberculosis. You should check the immunisation requirements with the universities and colleges you have chosen.

If you intend to apply for career-related courses, such as law or veterinary science, work experience may be an essential prerequisite for entry. You should check this well before applying to give you time to acquire it if necessary.

Students with certain disabilities may also be offered different entry requirements – it is worth checking with admissions tutors for individual courses as the criteria for admission may be relaxed.

How are entry requirements expressed?

Entry requirements may be expressed as specific grades (e.g. ABC at A level or ABBB at Scottish Higher), as a target number of UCAS Tariff points (e.g. 120 points) or as a mixture of the two (e.g. 120 points, including at least grade B in A level Chemistry).

> **TIP!**
>
> Entry requirements are listed in each course's entry in the UCAS search tool. Check these before you apply and keep checking, as requirements are subject to change!

The UCAS Tariff

The UCAS Tariff is the system for allocating points to qualifications used for entry to higher education.

As if the number of qualifications available were not confusing enough, different qualifications can have different grading structures (alphabetical, numerical or a mixture of both). Finding out what qualifications are needed for different higher education courses can be very confusing. So, the Tariff allows students to use a range of different qualifications to help secure a place on an undergraduate course.

Admission to higher education courses generally depends on an individual's achievement in level 3 qualifications. The UCAS Tariff gives a points value to each of these. Also included in the Tariff are a number of other qualifications that can be counted to boost the points score.

Some universities and colleges use the UCAS Tariff to make comparisons between applicants with different qualifications. Tariff points are often used in entry requirements, although other factors are often taken into account as well. Entry details (available from UCAS and on the institutions' own websites) provide a fuller picture of what admissions tutors are seeking.

The tables on pages 58–62 show the points values for the most common qualifications covered by the UCAS Tariff. To see the points values for other qualifications you may hold or be studying for, you should visit www.ucas.com/tariff, and search for the qualification.

You can find the Tariff tables at: www.ucas.com/tariff. You can also use the UCAS Tariff calculator there to find out how may points your qualifications and grades are allocated.

> **TIP!**
>
> If you have (or are likely to achieve) less than the minimum qualifications for entry to an honours degree course, your qualification level may be suitable for entry to an HND course or foundation degree, which you can convert into a full degree with an additional year of study (see Chapter 4 for further information).

Further information on the Tariff

Although Tariff points can be accumulated in a variety of ways, not all of these will necessarily be acceptable for entry to a particular higher education course. The achievement of a points score does not, therefore, give you an automatic right to a place, and admissions staff take many other factors into account when selecting students. The UCAS search tool at www.ucas.com is the best source of reference for which qualifications are acceptable for entry to specific courses.

How does the Tariff work?

- Students can collect Tariff points from a range of different qualifications.
- There is no ceiling to the number of points that can be accumulated.
- There is no double counting. Certain qualifications in the Tariff build on qualifications in the same subject that also attract Tariff points. Tariff points are generally only counted for the highest level of achievement in a subject. This means that you can't usually count AS grades if you have an A level in the same subject.
- UCAS Tariff points are allocated to Level 3/SCQF Level 6 qualifications.
- Where the Tariff refers to specific awarding bodies, only qualifications from these awarding bodies attract Tariff points.
- Qualifications with a similar title but from a different awarding body do not attract Tariff points.

UCAS Tariff Points tables

A levels and AS

Grade					
GCE & AVCE Double Award	A level with additional AS	GCE A level and AVCE	GCE AS Double Award	GCE AS & AS VCE	Tariff points
A*A*					112
A*A					104
AA					96
AB					88
BB					80
	A*A				76
BC					72
	AA				68
CC	AB				64
CD	BB	A*			56
	BC				52
DD		A			48
	CC				44
	CD				42
DE		B	AA		40
			AB		36
	DD				34
EE		C	BB		32
	DE				30
			BC		28
		D	CC		24
	EE		CD		22
			DD	A	20
		E	DE	B	16
			EE	C	12
				D	10
				E	6

Scottish Highers/Advanced Highers

Grade	Higher	Advanced Higher
A	33	56
B	27	48
C	21	40
D	15	32

Advanced Welsh Baccalaureate – Skills Challenge Certificate (first teaching September 2015 and first award 2017)

Grade	Tariff points
A*	56
A	48
B	40
C	32
D	24
E	16

Irish Leaving Certificate

Grade		Tariff points
Higher	Ordinary	
A1		36
A2		30
B1		30
B2		24
B3		24
C1		18
C2		18
C3	A1	12
D1		12
	A2	10
	B1	10
D2		9
D3		9
	B2	8
	B3	8
	C1	6
	C2	6

International Baccalaureate (IB) Diploma

While the IB Diploma does not attract UCAS Tariff points, the constituent qualifications of the IB Diploma do, so the total Tariff points for an IB Diploma can be calculated by adding together each of the following four components:

IB Certificate in Higher Level

Grade	Tariff points
H7	56
H6	48
H5	32
H4	24
H3	12
H2	0
H1	0

Size band: 4
Grade bands: 3–14

IB Certificate in Standard Level

Grade	Tariff points
S7	28
S6	24
S5	16
S4	12
S3	6
S2	0
S1	0

Size band: 2
Grade bands: 3–14

IB Certificate in Extended Essay

Grade	Tariff points
A	12
B	10
C	8
D	6
E	4

Size band: 1
Grade bands: 4–12

IB Certificate in Theory of Knowledge

Grade	Tariff points
A	12
B	10
C	8
D	6
E	4

Size band: 1
Grade bands: 4–12
Certificates in Extended Essay and Theory of Knowledge are awarded Tariff points when the certificates have been taken individually.

Cambridge International Pre-U Certificate

Grade	Principal Subject	Global Perspective and Research	Short Course
D1	56	56	22
D2	56	56	20
D3	52	52	20
M1	44	44	18
M2	40	40	14
M3	36	36	12
P1	28	28	10
P2	24	24	8
P3	20	20	6

Progression Diploma

Grade	Tariff points
A*	168
A	144
B	120
C	96
D	72
E	48

Extended Project – Stand alone

Grade	Tariff points
A*	28
A	24
B	20
C	16
D	12
E	8

Music examinations

Performance			Theory			Tariff points
Grade 8	Grade 7	Grade 6	Grade 8	Grade 7	Grade 6	
D						30
M						24
P						18
	D					16
	M	D				12
	P	M	D			10
			M			9
			P	D		8
				M		7
		P		P	D	6
					M	5
					P	4

Additional points will be awarded for music examinations from the Associated Board of the Royal Schools of Music (ABRSM), University of West London, Rockschool and Trinity Guildhall/Trinity College London (music examinations at grades 6, 7, 8 (D=Distinction; M=Merit; P=Pass)).

NB Full acknowledgement is made to UCAS for this information. For further details of all qualifications awarded UCAS Tariff points see www.ucas.com/tariff. Note that new qualifications are introduced each year.

How does higher education use the Tariff?

Not all qualifications attract UCAS Tariff points. The universities or colleges that interest you may accept your qualifications even if they don't attract UCAS Tariff points.

Not all institutions use the UCAS Tariff. Most prefer to express their entry requirements and make offers in terms of qualifications and grades rather than in Tariff points. Around one-third of course entry requirements make reference to the Tariff.

The courses that refer to UCAS Tariff points in their entry requirements do so in different ways:

- some list their entry requirements and make offers using only Tariff points, with no reference to specific qualifications or grades
- some ask for specific qualifications and a set number of Tariff points
- some link the Tariff points required to specific qualifications and grades. Examples include:
  - 120 points to include a grade B in A level History
  - 120 points including SQA Higher grade B in mathematics
  - 120 points. A levels, Scottish Highers and BTEC National Diplomas are acceptable qualifications

- 120 points. Points from General Studies A level, AS exams, key skills and COPE will not be considered
- 120 points gained from at least three A levels or equivalent 18 unit qualifications
- 120 points including A levels Mathematics and Physics.

Use of the Tariff may also vary from department to department at any one university or college, and may in some cases depend on the programme being offered.

Unit grade information

There is space for you to fill in your unit grade scores on your UCAS application – but you do not have to do so. (See under **Which qualifications to include?** in Chapter 15.) Unit grades may be specified as part of conditional offers, but this practice is not widespread.

You should look at individual university and college prospectuses and websites and check entry requirements and profiles to find out their individual policies relating to unit grade information.

Subjects

It is very important to check the combination of advanced-level subjects that is acceptable for admission to particular courses. This is a very thorny subject! Some departments, particularly at some of the UK's older universities, prefer the more traditional A level, Scottish Higher and IB subjects for the minimum entry requirement to some courses.

The list below shows the most commonly approved subjects:

- anthropology
- archaeology
- biology
- citizenship
- classical civilisation
- classical languages
- chemistry
- communication studies
- computing
- drama and theatre studies
- economics
- English (English language, English literature, and English language and literature)
- environmental studies/science
- further mathematics
- geography
- geology
- government and politics
- history

- history of art
- ICT
- law
- modern languages
- mathematics
- music
- philosophy
- physics
- psychology
- religious studies
- sociology
- statistics.

As a rule of thumb, subjects that may have overlapping content, such as business studies and economics, citizenship and government and politics, or chemistry or physics with physical science, are acceptable indiviudally but as a pair are less likely to be acceptable.

Some universities publish lists of the subjects they accept for entry and one group of 24 universities known as the Russell Group acts together by producing a list of *facilitating subjects* on behalf of all its members. These are the ones that are always acceptable and facilitate entry to a wide range of courses. They and many other universities would expect you to offer at least two from this list which follows:

- English literature
- history
- modern languages – e.g. French, German, Spanish, etc.
- classical languages – e.g. Latin, Ancient Greek
- maths and further maths
- physics
- biology
- chemistry
- geography.

Generally speaking, if you are taking two or more of the following subjects (and related titles) at advanced level, even though each one may be approved individually, you should check that the combination will be acceptable for entry to the higher education courses you are considering:

- accounting
- applied science
- art
- creative writing
- dance
- design and technology
- drama
- environmental science

- film studies
- general studies
- health & social care
- leisure studies
- media studies
- music technology
- performing arts
- photography
- physical education
- sports studies.

However, for many specialised or career-related degree and diploma programmes two or more subjects from the above list would be perfect!

So, to repeat, it is essential to check the exact entry requirements for any course you are considering.

There are no standard university-wide lists available, so the only way to clarify this is by consulting the admissions requirements for the course you would like to do.

Targeting the right courses

Here are a few dos and don'ts to make sure that the final five courses you select are targeted to give you the best chance of success.

Do ...

- Read course descriptions very carefully. Remember that courses with similar titles can have very different contents. This can affect the subjects required for entry.
- Carefully check the required entry grades and qualifications on the UCAS website, then confirm them by checking the universities' or colleges' prospectuses or websites. If you are unsure on any point contact the institutions directly to ensure that there is no chance you have misunderstood or to ask whether any changes have been made since the information was written.
- Check that the post-16 qualifications you have opted to take will give you the entry qualifications you need and that you are on track to achieve the right grades.
- Be realistic about the grades you are likely to achieve. Make sure that you know what exam grades teachers are going to predict for you.
- As a safety net, make sure you apply to at least one course that is likely to give you a slightly lower offer.

Don't ...

- Apply for lots of different or unrelated subjects: you will have a difficult job justifying this in your personal statement, and admissions tutors will question how genuine your interest is in each subject.
- Even if you expect high grades, think very carefully before applying to five very popular universities for a very popular subject. Entry will be extremely competitive and, even with high predicted grades, you cannot be sure of being accepted. Better to include at least one university or college that is not so oversubscribed, and therefore makes offers at a slightly lower level.

Resources

Publications

- *Choose the Right A Levels*, Trotman Education, www.trotman. co.uk.
- *Choosing Your Degree Course & University*, Trotman Education, www.trotman.co.uk.
- *Heap 2019: University Degree Course Offers*, Trotman Education, www.trotman.co.uk.

Websites

- www.ucas.com.
- www.push.co.uk.
- www.theguardian.com/education/universityguide.
- www.telegraph.co.uk/education/universities-colleges.
- www.thecompleteuniversityguide.co.uk.
- www.timeshighereducation.com.
- www.gov.uk/government/organisations/disclosure-and-barring-service: criminal records check in England and Wales.
- www.justice-ni.gov.uk: criminal records check in Northern Ireland.
- www.mygov.scot/basic-disclosure/apply-for-basic-disclosure: criminal records check in Scotland.

Part II

The admissions procedure: applications, interviews, offers and beyond

7| Applications and offers

Making your application

As the timetable on pages 3–6 shows, if you are on a two-year advanced course, all your higher education research work should ideally be done by September or October of the second year – more than a year before you start in higher education.

If you are on a one-year course, you won't have time to do all the activities suggested for the first year, but you are working to the same application deadlines and you still need to research all your options.

UCAS applicant journey

The UCAS applicant journey (see Figure 1, page 70) has been designed to guide you through the different steps you will take when making your application for higher education.

Deadlines

There are three deadlines for applications to courses through UCAS. They are 18.00 hours (UK time) on each of these dates: 15 October, 15 January and 24 March.

The deadline for application to most courses is 18.00 hours (UK time), 15 January. (Remember, however, that you will have to submit your application to your referee well before this.) All applications submitted by 15 January are considered – however, it is advisable to apply as early as you can. This is because too many people apply after Christmas, during the two weeks leading up to the 15 January deadline; those who apply earlier may therefore receive a quicker decision simply because smaller numbers are being handled. Aim to submit your UCAS application to your referee by late November or by any internal deadline given by your school or college. You may apply after 15 January and universities and colleges may consider your application if they still have places – but they are not obliged to do so. Any applications received after 30 June will be referred to Clearing. However, if you are applying from outside the EU you may apply until 30 June without being regarded as a late applicant.

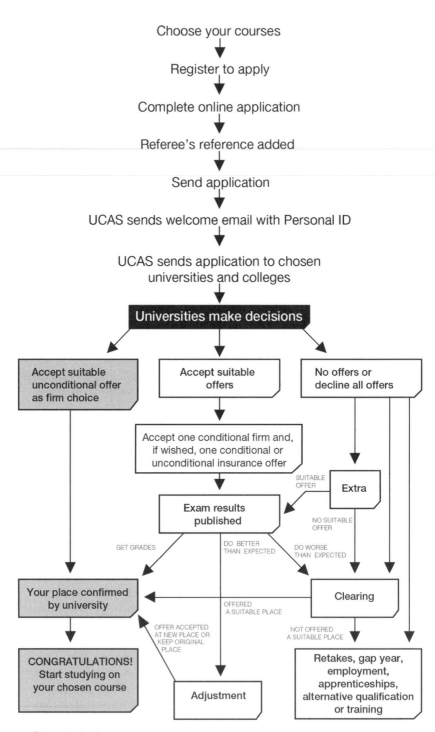

Figure 1: Applicant journey

Some courses have an earlier application deadline:

- applications for courses leading to professional qualifications in medicine, dentistry or veterinary science/medicine must be submitted by 18.00 hours (UK time) on 15 October
- applications for all courses at the universities of Oxford or Cambridge must be submitted by 18.00 hours (UK time) on 15 October.

These deadlines apply to all students, including those from outside the EU.

Some subjects have a later deadline:

- the deadline for the receipt at UCAS of applications for art and design courses, except those listed with a 15 January deadline, is 18.00 hours (UK time) on 24 March. (If you apply for art and design courses with different deadlines, you can submit your application before 15 January for courses with that deadline, then add further choices before the 24 March deadline, unless you have already used all five choices. The reason for the later deadline is to allow students who are on a Diploma in Art and Design, Foundation Studies course to have enough time to decide on a specialism and prepare a portfolio of work which they will have to present at interview. Deadlines for individual courses can all be found in the universities' and colleges' own information and also by using the UCAS search tool.)

What happens once you submit your application?

UCAS will send you a welcome email acknowledging receipt of your application and confirming your personal details and the courses you have applied for. You must check that this information is correct, and contact the UCAS Customer Experience Centre immediately if it is not (0371 486 0 468, between 08.30 and 18.00, Monday to Friday, or +44 330 3330 230 from outside the UK).

UCAS will also provide you with your Personal ID. Along with the password you used for Apply (see Chapter 11), this will enable you to log in to the UCAS database and use Track (the online tracking system) to follow the progress of your application. Keep a careful note of your Personal ID and, if you contact UCAS, universities or colleges, be prepared to quote it – this will save a lot of time and trouble.

Admissions tutors can now look at your application and decide whether to make you an offer.

Decisions and offers

Universities and colleges will inform UCAS of their decisions. You should log in to Track periodically to check the status of your application. In addition, UCAS will email you to tell you that a change has been made to your application status. The message will not specify whether you have received an offer or a rejection, but will ask you to log in to Track to find out.

Decisions will arrive in a random order, possibly beginning a few weeks after you apply. Decisions will be displayed in Track as soon as UCAS receives them. If you have a long wait, it may mean that an admissions tutor is under great pressure due to a large number of applications. So, do not worry if people you know receive offers while you are still waiting to hear; it does not necessarily mean bad news.

There are three main categories of decision.

1. **Unconditional offer**: no further qualifications are required. If you accept this offer, and meet all non-academic requirements (DBS and health checks for example), you are in!
2. **Conditional offer**: you still have some work to do ... but if you accept the offer and achieve the conditions in the examinations you are about to take, a place will be guaranteed.
3. **Unsuccessful**: sorry – no luck. However, it may be that you receive an offer from one of your other choices. If all decisions are unsuccessful, you should not feel discouraged, as there is still the option of applying to courses through UCAS Extra and Clearing.

The following decisions may also appear:

* withdrawn: you have withdrawn this choice
* cancelled: you have asked UCAS to cancel this choice.

Universities and colleges have to decide by 2 May whether to offer you a place, provided you applied by the deadline of 15 January. (They are encouraged to make their decisions by 31 March.)

Interviews and open days

Before they make a decision, admissions tutors may wish to call you for interview. You should therefore be prepared to travel to universities or colleges during the late autumn and winter; a 16–25 Railcard or a National Express Young Persons Coachcard might be a good investment.

Some universities and colleges will contact you directly to invite you for interview. Others will inform you of interview details through Track on the UCAS website. If you are invited for interview through Track, UCAS will send you an email asking you to look at the change to your application in Track. You can accept the interview invitation, decline it or request an alternative date or time in Track.

If you need to change the interview time or date, you should also contact the university or college direct. They can then update the invitation so that the revised details are shown in Track. You should try to attend interviews on the first date given as it may be difficult for admissions tutors to offer an alternative date.

Advice on preparing for interviews is given in Chapter 9.

Alternatively, you may be offered a conditional or unconditional place and invited to attend an open day. You might also be asked to submit a portfolio or piece of written work.

Replying to offers

You will be asked to reply to any offers you receive – and you must do so – but you do not have to reply until you have received decisions from all the universities and colleges to which you applied. UCAS will send you a statement listing all your offers (and/or rejections) and will give you a deadline for replying. This may be different from the deadlines received by your friends. Do not worry about this. There is no one single deadline; UCAS acts only after you have heard from all your choices.

You can reply to your offers using Track on the UCAS website. You must reply to each offer with one of three options.

1. **Firm acceptance**: if you firmly accept an offer (either as an unconditional offer or as a conditional offer), this means that you are sure that this offer is your first preference of all the offers you have received through UCAS. If you get the grades, this will be the higher education course you take. You can make this reply only once; you will not subsequently be able to change or cancel your reply. There is also an equal commitment on the university's or college's part to accept you if you fulfil the conditions.
2. **Insurance acceptance**: if you have firmly accepted a conditional offer, you may also hold one additional offer (either conditional or unconditional) as an insurance acceptance. This is your fall-back, in case your grades are too low for your firm acceptance. It is worth knowing that you are not obliged to make an insurance reply; if you do so and then your firm acceptance offer is not confirmed, you will be expected to attend your insurance choice if that is confirmed. If you cannot feel 100% committed to your insurance choice it would be better to wait and see what is available in Clearing. Please ask for advice before making this decision!
3. **Decline**: if you decline an offer, you are indicating that you definitely do not wish to accept it.

You must either accept or decline your offers. You can accept two offers (your firm and insurance choices) and must decline all your other offers, so your combination of replies will be one of the following:

- accept one offer firmly (unconditional firm or conditional firm) and decline any others
- accept one offer firmly (conditional firm) and one as an insurance (unconditional insurance or conditional insurance), and decline any others
- decline all offers.

If you firmly accept an unconditional offer of a place, you are not entitled to choose an insurance offer.

If you firmly accept a conditional offer, you may accept an unconditional offer or another conditional offer as your insurance acceptance.

> ### TIP!
>
> Do not worry if people you know receive replies before you do. This does not mean that you are going to be rejected. Some admissions tutors, for various reasons, take longer to deal with applications than others.

Tips on making your replies

- Consider your replies very carefully. Ask for advice from your school/college tutor or careers adviser.
- Do not accept an offer (firm or insurance) unless you are sure that you will be happy to enrol on the course. The decisions you make are binding; you are not permitted to alter your choices at a later stage *unless* you find that you have done better than you expected at exam results time and have higher grades than those required by your firm choice. You may then choose to use Adjustment (see Chapter 10).
- It is advisable to choose an unconditional offer as your insurance acceptance or one with conditions that are easier for you to meet than those of your firm acceptance.
- Do not include as an insurance acceptance a course that you would be unwilling to take up. If you are not accepted for your firm choice and the insurance offer is confirmed, you are committed to going there. It would be better not to hold an insurance acceptance than to hold one you would not be willing to take up.
- Bear in mind the precise requirements of the offer. For example, if a BCC offer requires a B in a subject you are not very confident about, but an offer requiring higher grades overall does not specify the B in that subject or perhaps counts general studies, then your firm/insurance decision needs to take these factors into account.

What if you don't get any offers?

If you are in this position, you may be able to make a further application in Extra between 25 February and 18.00 hours (UK time) on 4 July. In 2017, 6,370 people were accepted through the Extra route. This was a decrease of 15% from the previous year.

You will be eligible to use Extra if you have used all five choices in your original application and you fulfil any one of the following criteria:

- you have had unsuccessful or withdrawn decisions for all your choices
- you have cancelled your outstanding choices and hold no offers
- you have received decisions from all five choices and have declined all offers made to you.

> **TIP!**
>
> If you applied to only one course and you have not accepted or declined your offers you have the option of adding more choices through Track before 30 June. You will have to pay the additional £6 application fee.

If you are eligible to use Extra, UCAS will notify you of this. When you log in to Track, you will see that a special Extra button becomes available on your screen. You will still be able to search for courses that still have vacancies in the UCAS search tool on the website. You may apply for several courses – but only one at a time.

> **TIP!**
>
> It is a good idea to contact the admissions tutors for the courses that interest you and ask whether they will consider you.

When you enter the Extra course details on your Track screen, your application is automatically sent online to the relevant university or college.

If you are made an offer, you can then choose whether to accept it. If you are currently studying for examinations, any offer that you receive is likely to be a conditional one and will contain the required exam grades. If you decide to accept a conditional offer, you will not be able to take any further part in Extra. (There are no insurance options in Extra.) If you already have your exam results, you may receive an unconditional offer. Once you accept an unconditional offer, you have that place.

If you are unsuccessful, decline an offer or do not receive an offer *within 21 days of choosing a course* through Extra, you can (time permitting) make a further application in Extra. The Extra button on your Track screen will be re-activated.

Tips on using Extra

- Do some careful research and seek guidance from your school, college or careers adviser and from the universities and colleges themselves.
- Think very carefully before applying again for the types of course for which you have already been unsuccessful – it may simply result in another rejection.
- Be flexible – for example, if you applied to high-demand courses and universities and colleges in your original application and were unsuccessful, you could consider related or alternative subjects.
- If you're not offered a place in Extra, you may still find a place through Clearing (see page 103, Chapter 10).
- You can find out more about Extra on the UCAS website, at www. ucas.com/extra.

8 | Non-standard applications

Applications for the majority of courses follow the pattern outlined in the previous chapters. However, there are some exceptions, specifically for:

- courses at the universities of Oxford and Cambridge
- music conservatoires
- medicine, dentistry and veterinary science or veterinary medicine courses
- mature students
- deferred entry
- late applications
- international students.

Oxford and Cambridge

If you intend to apply for any course at either Oxford or Cambridge, the deadline for submitting your application is 18.00 hours (UK time) on 15 October 2018. (Additional forms must be submitted at an earlier date if you wish to be considered for a music or choral scholarship at either university. You can find details on their websites.)

The four Cambridge colleges for mature students – Hughes Hall, Lucy Cavendish (women only), St Edmund's and Wolfson – consider applications from mature students (defined as over 21 years of age) for some subjects as part of a second application round until 1 March. Architecture, history of art, medicine, music, philosophy and veterinary science are excluded from this scheme and must meet the standard deadlines.

Certain applicants to the University of Cambridge must also submit a Cambridge Online Preliminary Application (COPA) form as well as a UCAS application. They are:

- those living outside the EU at the time of application
- those attending school/college/university outside the EU at the time of application
- those wishing to be considered for an organ scholarship.

Shortly after submitting your UCAS application, you will be asked via email to complete an online Supplementary Application Questionnaire (SAQ). You must submit your SAQ by the deadline set. In the majority of cases this deadline will be 18.00 hours (UK time) on 22 October 2018.

The purpose of the SAQ, Cambridge says, is to ensure that admissions tutors have consistent information about all applicants. It also permits them to collect information that is not part of the UCAS application such as the topics students have covered as part of A level (or equivalent) courses and helps the interviewers decide which questions to ask.

Cambridge interviews are conducted in certain countries (Canada, China, Hong Kong, India, Malaysia and Singapore). If you want to take advantage of this scheme, rather than come to Cambridge, you must consult the list of dates on the website. However, applicants invited for interview for architecture, history of art, classics and music are advised to travel to Cambridge for interview.

Most applicants to the University of Oxford are not required to submit a separate form, but extra information is required for some international interviews, and choral and organ award applicants must submit an additional form online by 1 September 2018.

You can apply to only one course at *either* the University of Oxford or the University of Cambridge. You cannot apply to both universities. There is only one exception to this: if you will be a graduate at the start of the course and are applying for course code A101 (graduate medicine) at the University of Cambridge, you can also apply to medicine (course code A100) at Cambridge, in addition to being able to apply to graduate medicine (course code A101) at the University of Oxford. No other combinations are permitted, however those applying for organ awards can audition at both universities.

Some applicants will need to complete an additional application form. For full information about applying to the universities of Oxford or Cambridge, please visit their websites at www.ox.ac.uk or www.study.cam.ac.uk. In-depth advice on making applications to these universities is also given in *Getting into Oxford & Cambridge* (Trotman Education).

Applying to study at a conservatoire

You can apply for performance-based music, dance, drama and musical theatre courses at nine UK conservatoires online using the UCAS Conservatoires scheme, which is run by UCAS and works in a similar way. However, applicants can select six courses rather than the five possible through the UCAS Undergraduate scheme. The application fee for UCAS Conservatoires is £25 and there are also audition fees to pay.

The nine conservatoires are:

1. Royal Birmingham Conservatoire
2. Bristol Old Vic Theatre School
3. Leeds College of Music (undergraduate courses through UCAS and postgraduate course through UCAS Conservatoires)

4. Royal Academy of Music
5. Royal College of Music
6. Royal Conservatoire of Scotland
7. Royal Northern College of Music
8. Royal Welsh College of Music and Drama
9. Trinity Laban Conservatoire of Music and Dance.

If you are applying for music courses, you can choose either a joint course (50/50), a major/minor course (75/25) or you can provide two options, either of which you would be happy to study.

You can apply for music, dance, drama and musical theatre courses from mid-July 2018.

For music courses the application deadline is 18.00 hours (UK time) on 1 October 2018, although late entries may be considered if there are vacancies.

For most dance, drama and musical theatre courses the deadline is 15 January 2019. However, there are some exceptions, particularly for certain audition locations and for international applicants so it is important to check the conservatoire websites for full details.

Applying to UCAS Conservatoires does not mean that you are excluded from the UCAS Undergraduate system. The two systems run independently of each other, therefore you may also make up to five choices through UCAS Undergraduate. However – you may only accept a place through one system.

Three conservatoires (members of the organisation Conservatoires UK) do not recruit through UCAS Conservatoires. They use either the standard UCAS scheme or run their own independent admissions systems.They are:

- The Conservatoire for Dance and Drama (a group of eight specialist colleges)
- Guildhall School of Music and Drama
- Royal Central School of Speech and Drama.

Auditions preparation advice (music applicants)

Research
Check the **required audition repertoire**, and start to study it as far ahead as possible of the audition period, which is usually November/December. An audition is not the platform to try out a new piece! If you also play something of your own choice, select something in consultation with your teacher which shows you at your best and which you enjoy playing.

Your **personal statement** should be about your aspirations, feelings about music and your experience. Showing understanding of today's music profession, which is competitive and requires versatility, is helpful and indicates a suitable temperament. One of your references should be your specialist instrumental/vocal/composition teacher, as they can give a professional indication of work-in-progress.

Have several '**practice auditions**' to family and friends – include walking into the room, settling down and performing in unfamiliar settings. Playing from memory is not required by all conservatoires, but no musician should be 'glued' to the music. An accompanist will normally be provided but rehearsal may be limited. You should be completely familiar with the piano part.

Practical considerations
Presentation is an important element of performance. Wear smart, comfortable clothes that you can play in with ease.

- On entering the room, smile at the panel. They will want you to do your best.
- Demonstrate an understanding of context of your music by pronouncing the names and composers of your pieces correctly. Tune carefully, quickly and quietly to the piano in the room.
- Don't be disconcerted if you don't play everything; the panel may want to talk to you for longer.
- They are looking for potential and temperament – not a completed artist. Engage and interest the panel, keeping your performance fresh, with a wide dynamic range and sense of changes of mood and colour.
- Maintain musical interest in your repertoire – it is easy to slide into staleness. Avoid this! Try to demonstrate an interest in conveying the intentions of a composer and a love for the medium in which you are working. Panels can differentiate between mishaps caused by nerves, and elements of playing that are undeveloped.
- The interview questions may be about your performance and to see how good your critical faculties are. Think about this in advance.

Source: Royal Northern College of Music, www.rncm.ac.uk/study-here/how-to-apply/audition-process/audition-preparation-advice.

Please note that the information is correct as of 26 February 2018, but may be subject to change, so ensure to check the website (www.rncm.ac.uk) for the most up-to-date information.

Medicine, dentistry and veterinary science/ veterinary medicine courses

If you intend to apply for a course leading to a professional qualification in medicine, dentistry or veterinary science/medicine, the deadline for submitting your application is 18.00 hours (UK time) on 15 October 2018. You are allowed to select a maximum of four courses in any one of these subjects: if you list more than four, Apply (the UCAS application system described fully in Part III) will ask you to reduce your number of choices. The remaining space on your UCAS application can be filled with a course in another subject, should you so wish. There is strong competition for entry to medicine, dentistry and veterinary science/ medicine courses and many people are necessarily disappointed in their first choice of study.

In-depth advice on making applications in these subject areas is given in the *Getting into* series (see the 'Resources' section at the end of this chapter).

Mature students

There is no single definition of a 'mature' applicant, but most universities and colleges now classify students as 'mature' if they are over 21 years of age at the date of entry to a course. The vast majority of departments welcome applications from mature students, and many, especially science departments, would like more.

As a mature student, you are more likely to be accepted with qualifications that would not be good enough if they were presented by a student aged 18 who is in full-time education. That said, there is still fierce competition for places, and in most subjects places are not set aside for mature students. If you are considered favourably, you are likely to be called for interview. It is not usually advisable to rely only on qualifications gained several years ago at school; university and college departments will probably want to see recent evidence of your academic ability so that they can evaluate your application fairly. In addition, taking a course of study at the right level helps prepare you for full-time student life.

It is also very important if you are applying for courses leading to any of the caring professions or those related to medicine that you can demonstrate relevant work experience.

Admissions tutors for courses that interest you will be able to advise you. If they do expect evidence of recent study they might suggest for instance that you go to a further education college and study for one of the usual post-16 qualifications (e.g. an A level, Higher or National Award) or take one of the Access to Higher Education or foundation courses specially designed for mature students.

You may also find that, through what is known as *Accreditation of Prior Learning* (APL), you can obtain acceptance of alternative qualifications or, through *Accreditation of Prior Experiential Learning* (APEL), acceptance of some of the skills you have developed in the workplace. You will need to contact universities and colleges direct to find out what their policies are.

Definitions:

- Accreditation of Prior Learning (also known as Recognition of Prior Learning) is essentially credit awarded for wider learning gained through self-directed study, work or training. It is a process used by many organisations, including higher education institutions, around the world, to evaluate skills and knowledge acquired outside formal education. Methods of assessing prior learning are varied and include: evaluation of experience gained through volunteer work, previous paid or unpaid employment, or observation of actual workplace behaviour.
- Accreditation of Prior Experiential Learning (APEL) is an extension of APL that includes assessed learning gained from life and work experience. APEL is similar to APL in that it is recognition of prior learning but is broader as it allows, in theory, for learning from any prior experience. Often APEL and APL are used synonymously and the terms overlap.

TIPS!

Evidence of relevant work experience will boost your application and show that you know what you are committing to.

Evidence of previous study will show that you will be able to cope with the academic content of the course.

It is advisable for mature students to contact departments directly to ask about their admissions policies before applying to UCAS and to tailor their applications accordingly.

Deferred entry

Taking a gap year is an increasingly popular option for many students – it offers a unique opportunity to broaden horizons, travel, work as a volunteer and/or (as the cost of higher education continues to rise) save some money while gaining valuable experience in the workplace. If you do plan, for whatever reason, to defer your entry into higher education until 2020, there are three options available to you – each is listed below with a few notes on the pros and cons.

Option 1: apply through UCAS for deferred entry

You can make your application this year and select a start date of 2020 in your UCAS application to indicate that you wish to defer your entry (see Chapter 14). The major advantage of this option is that you get the formalities out of the way while you are still at school or college and available for interview – then you can relax. It's important to note that you will still have to meet the terms of offers made to you even though you will be delaying entry.

Generally speaking, applications for deferred entry are dealt with in the normal way, but do be aware that for some subjects (such as medicine, certain science and mathematics subjects and professional subjects) admissions tutors may be a little cautious about offering you a place. (They say that they want to be sure that your skills and knowledge are really up to date – that you have not forgotten what you learned during your advanced course!) It is therefore important to be sure you really want to defer before using this option, and to check with the department to which you are thinking of applying whether it would be happy to admit you a year later.

Remember that if you do apply for entry in 2020 but then find that you have no useful way of spending the gap year after all, the university or college is not obliged to take you a year earlier (i.e. in 2019). If you choose to defer, remember to mention your reasons and plans for your year out in the personal statement section of Apply (see Chapter 17): this is much more likely to make admissions tutors willing to give you a deferred place.

Option 2: apply through UCAS for standard entry

If you are not confident enough of your decision to apply for deferred entry on your UCAS application, you can apply for the normal admission year and, later on, ask the university or college where you are accepted whether you can defer. This means you do not need to say anything on your UCAS application about deferred entry. However, the university or college is quite entitled to say that the place it has offered you is for 2019 entry only, and you must either take it up or apply all over again for entry in 2020.

Option 3: do not apply through UCAS until the following year

It is possible to delay applying to UCAS until after you have received your results, which means that you make your UCAS application during your gap year. This can be a good option in some instances, especially if your exam results turn out to be significantly different from those that were predicted. Your grades are also guaranteed, and if you accept an offer it will be a firm decision, so universities and colleges may consider you a better bet than a candidate who is only predicted those grades. The disadvantage, though, is that you must find time during your gap year to get your research up to date, fill in your UCAS application and (possibly) attend open days and interviews. This can limit your gap year options – you will need to be contactable at all times, and flying back from Australia (or wherever else you decide to spend your gap year) to attend an interview could make a serious dent in your finances!

Making a late application

If at all possible, avoid applying late. Many popular courses fill up quickly, and getting a place will be more difficult, if not impossible. However, if you decide you would like to apply to higher education late, you still can. Up to 30 June, UCAS will send your application to your named institutions, but the universities and colleges will consider you only at their discretion. If they do choose to consider you, the same procedures are followed as for a normal application, and you will reply to offers in the usual way. Applications received between 1 July and 20 September will be processed through the Clearing scheme, which operates from mid-July to late September.

International students

If you are an international student – i.e. resident outside the EU – the general information given in this chapter and in Chapter 7 applies to you. However, UCAS has some specific additional advice for you.

- Make sure you add all the qualifications you have or are currently working for. Visit www.ucas.com/fillinginyourapplication for advice on entering qualifications on your application.
- Give as much information as possible; without it, admissions tutors will struggle to make a decision.
- You may have to send proof of your results in certificates or transcripts to the universities or colleges. They all have different policies on how they want to receive them. While some of them ask you to send everything straight away, others will do their initial assessment of your application before asking to see proof of your results.
- Although UCAS can send some results from the awarding bodies to your chosen universities and colleges – including the International Baccalaureate – for most international qualifications you will have to send them direct to universities and colleges yourself.
- Follow the advice in Chapter 17 for your personal statement, but also say why you want to study in the UK, describe your English language skills (and mention any English courses or tests you have

taken) and explain why you want to be an international student rather than study in your own country.

As mentioned in Chapter 7, your deadline for application is 30 June (although you are advised to apply as early as possible) but for courses listed on page 71 you must observe the same (earlier) deadlines as EU students.

You will find a lot of useful information on the UCAS website on costs of study here, visas and student life in the UK.

Visa requirements

Currently, students from non-EU countries must have a valid visa in order to be able to study for a degree in the UK. However, there are exemptions for students from certain countries; full details are available on the government website (www.gov.uk/check-uk-visa).

Universities each set their own academic and English language requirements for international students, and you will need an offer of a university place before you can begin your visa application. In order to obtain a visa, the university that has made you an offer will need to act as a sponsor for your visa application. Once you have accepted the offer, the university will then give you a Confirmation of Acceptance for Studies (CAS) letter, after which you can apply for the visa. Note that you will also need to demonstrate that you have sufficient funds to cover the first year of tuition fees and living expenses; further details are available at www.ukcisa.org.uk.

Brexit

Following the UK's decision to leave the EU, visa arrangements for EU students applying to UK institutions are to be negotiated as part of wider discussions with the EU. However, for the time being, no visa restrictions apply for EU students.

Resources

Publications

- *Getting into Art & Design Courses*, Trotman Education, www.trotman.co.uk.
- *Getting into Dental School*, Trotman Education, www.trotman.co.uk.
- *Getting into Medical School 2019 Entry*, Trotman Education, www.trotman.co.uk.

- *Getting into Oxford & Cambridge 2019 Entry*, Trotman Education, www.trotman.co.uk.
- *Getting into Veterinary School*, Trotman Education, www.trotman. co.uk.
- *Heap 2019: University Degree Course Offers*, Trotman Education, www.trotman.co.uk.

Websites

- www.cam.ac.uk: for information on applications to Cambridge.
- www.ox.ac.uk: for information on applications to Oxford.
- www.ucas.com/conservatoires.
- www.ucas.com/trackyourapplication: to find out what happens after your apply.
- www.ucas.com/international-toolkit: includes a guide to applying to study in the UK in 13 different languages. Currently, languages are Arabic, Bulgarian, Chinese, French, German, Greek, Italian, Lithuanian, Norwegian, Polish, Romanian, Russian and Spanish.

9| Interviews and selection

In many cases, the decision to offer you a place will be made using the information you supplied on your application, but admissions tutors for several courses often require more detailed information about applicants. If this applies to you, you can expect to be asked to attend an interview or audition, or to take a written test.

Interviews

Many universities and colleges (especially the popular ones, running competitive courses) want to meet applicants and find out whether they would cope with the demands of the course before making an offer.

Admissions tutors are seeking able students with academic potential, in sufficient numbers to fill the places on their courses.

In deciding which applicants to accept, they are looking for the following.

- **Intellectual ability**: can you cope with the academic and professional demands of the subject and course?
- **Competition**: how well do you compare with other applicants for the course?
- **Applicants who are likely to accept**: if offered a place, is there a good chance that you will accept it?
- **Students who will make a contribution**: will you get involved in the life of the university or college and contribute in lectures, practicals and tutorials?
- **Applicants who are likely to get the grades**: are you expected to achieve the level of grades in your exams that this course generally commands?

And, very importantly!

- **Motivation**: a real and passionate interest in the subject.

They may be able to find much of this information in your personal statement (see Chapter 17), but some will also use interviews to help them decide which applicants to make an offer to. There is usually no standard policy throughout one institution. In most cases admissions tutors themselves decide whom to interview.

In general, interviews are still used:

- for borderline candidates: give it your best shot, because many admissions tutors like to give applicants a chance even when doubtful whether you will make the grade
- for applicants who have not studied the subject before: tutors need to know that you have researched it and know what it involves
- to distinguish between large numbers of similar, very able, applicants: this is particularly likely if you are applying for very competitive courses, for example at Oxbridge or other high-status universities or colleges
- for vocational courses: those that lead to a particular career, for example:
  - agriculture
  - dentistry
  - health and social care
  - medicine
  - nursing
  - healthcare professions, e.g. physiotherapy, radiography, dietetics or occupational therapy
  - social work
  - teaching
  - veterinary science.

The majority of the above courses lead to work in a caring profession – which is why admissions tutors particularly need to be able to assess a student's suitability for the career – but it is not unusual for applicants to courses in architecture or engineering to be interviewed, and they may also be asked to take examples of work or to talk about a project.

Universities and colleges that have a policy of calling applicants for interview may arrange to conduct interviews by telephone, video-conferencing or Skype for people who are unable to attend personally. This applies mainly to applicants who live outside the UK.

You may receive your invitation to an interview either in a personal letter or email or through Track. In all cases you will be offered a date and time. Instructions will be given on how to change these if they are inconvenient.

What will you be asked?

Interviews can take different forms – you could find yourself on your own in front of just one person or an interview panel; or in a group, being observed as you discuss a topic or carry out a particular task. You may even be asked to take a written test.

Interview questions can be wide ranging and unpredictable – but, on the other hand, there are a few that tend to come up over and over again. It

is wise to have considered how you might respond to predictable questions such as these:

- Why do you want to study this subject?
- Why have you applied to this department or faculty?
- Why have you chosen this university or college?
- What are your spare-time interests?
- Why should we offer you a place? (Tricky! Don't be modest.)
- Tell me about an achievement you are proud of.
- What have you read outside your syllabus?
- What skills do you consider to have gained from your part-time job?
- Tell me more about the sports team/voluntary work/drama group you described on your application.
- Have you any questions to ask?

You should also be prepared to talk about the following:

- your advanced-level study: what particularly interests you? What additional reading and research have you done?
- topical issues relating to your chosen subject
- anything you have mentioned in your personal statement.

In the case of vocational courses, you can expect to discuss anything you have done to gain useful experience, such as work experience in a hospital, care setting, architectural practice, engineering company, accountant's or solicitor's office. Be prepared to describe what you did, what you learned and how the experience helped you to decide on your higher education course.

Preparing yourself

Prepare as much as you can. Obviously you should not memorise or recite answers to any of the questions above – but think through the kind of things you would like to say. Taking the question 'Why should we give you a place?' as an example, you could:

- talk about your strengths, interests and ambitions, particularly with reference to courses you are interested in
- mention anything a bit individual or a little different that you can bring to share with others: for example, you may have debating experience, great rugby skills, extensive experience in charity fund-raising or orienteering expertise; or you may have developed men-toring skills through your work as a sixth-form or college ambassador to 11–16-year-olds.

It is a good idea to ask your school or college to give you a mock interview – preferably with a member of staff who does not know you. This can be an excellent way of preparing yourself to think on your feet and answer unexpected questions and you should get some helpful feedback.

You should start thinking about interviews as early as possible. As you consider your course choices and compile a shortlist of universities and colleges to apply to, you should research answers to the questions admissions tutors might ask. If the admissions tutor comes up with 'Why have you chosen this university or college?', you will then remember their particularly strong facilities or the unique angle of the course.

Try to keep interviews in mind as you write your personal statement (see Chapter 17). It is very likely that interviewers will use this as a basis for their questions, so do not mention anything you cannot talk about and expand on. And, if you have a particular passion or area of interest in your chosen subject that you are just dying to talk about, make sure you mention it in your statement.

Top tips for interviews

- Dress should be 'smart casual'. There is no need for it to be very formal. The interviewer probably won't be dressed formally either. As a general rule avoid jeans, and go for a skirt or smart trousers with a shirt, rather than a t-shirt.
- Make eye contact with the interviewer. If there is more than one interviewer always reply to the person who asked the question – but look at the other/s from time to time to include them in your answer.
- Do your best to show that you are thoughtful, committed and genuinely interested in your chosen subject.
- Always have one or two prepared questions of your own about the course, opportunities after you graduate or a relevant academic topic. (Don't ask questions only on topics covered in the material already published and sent to you by the university or college.)
- Make sure that you know exactly what you wrote in your personal statement.
- Don't bluff. If you don't know the answer to a question, ask the interviewer to repeat it or put it in a different way. If you still don't know, admit it!
- Most important – be sure that you know exactly how to get to the interview. Check your travel arrangements. Make sure that you are going to the correct site if the university or college has more than one. Allow plenty of time for your transport to be late and to find the right building and room when you get there.
- Take the interviewer's name and phone number with you so that you can call and explain if you are unavoidably delayed.

There are further useful tips on preparing for interviews and on what to expect on the UCAS website, www.ucas.com/invitations.

More detailed advice on interview technique and possible interview questions is given in the *Getting into* series (see the 'Resources' section below).

Auditions and portfolios

Your subject teachers will be able to offer more specific advice, but here are a few general points.

If you are applying for a performance-based course in drama, music, dance or musical theatre, you will have to attend an audition – usually before an interview. (Some applicants are weeded out at the audition stage.)

Policies vary at different institutions, but drama applicants can expect to be asked to:

- perform one or more pieces, often one from Shakespeare and one by a modern playwright – at some institutions, though, you are free to choose your own pieces
- deliver a monologue
- do some improvisation
- do some movement work
- work in a group.

You will be sent detailed instructions on what and how to prepare before your audition.

Music students can expect to have to:

- perform at least two (contrasting) pieces – often from a set list – sent to you in advance – but sometimes of your own choice
- sight read
- improvise
- do technical tests (scales and arpeggios).

Dance students can expect to have to:

- participate in one or more dance classes, observed by teaching staff
- improvise
- perform a short piece choreographed by themselves
- participate in a group interview
- have an interview with one or more people which focuses on their future ambitions.

Sometimes a physical examination is included.

Music, drama, dance and musical theatre applicants can benefit from performing for a small audience before attending an audition. Your teachers may organise this automatically and arrange for you to perform in front of them and other students. You should then receive some feedback and constructive criticism.

Auditions are usually held in two parts. A group of students attend a first audition, then some are selected to attend a second or recall one. This often happens on the same day so that students successful in the first audition do not have the expense of returning on another date.

Art students normally have to take a portfolio of work with them – and will be expected to talk about it. You might be asked questions by one or two individual interviewers or you might be expected to display your pieces like a mini exhibition and explain how you developed and changed a piece as you worked on it. The usual advice is to:

- include some work that you have done on your own, i.e. not as part of coursework
- include notebooks and sketches as well as finished work
- bring photographs of three-dimensional work that is too heavy to take with you.

You will be told what size your portfolio should be and how many pieces of work it should contain. However, some admissions tutors prefer to see portfolios in advance and assess them at the same time as they read the UCAS application. If so, you will receive a request (usually by email) for your portfolio. The email you receive will tell you how to submit your portfolio – and full instructions will be given if you are expected to do so online.

It is a good idea to ask your art teacher to give you a mock interview and ask you questions on your portfolio.

Applicants for film-making and screen courses are expected to submit a different type of portfolio. You may normally include still work – photographs and art work – but the major element will be a short film lasting just a few minutes. (Timing is very important. Films that overrun are not accepted.) You will be told whether you must use a set theme or may use your own, how many actors the film should include and whether you must use an indoor or outdoor location. You will be invited to explain your film and what you were aiming to achieve to the interview panel.

Aptitude tests

Many students now get straight A grades and admissions tutors for oversubscribed courses have no way of distinguishing between them. So several admissions tests have been devised to give them additional information that is relevant to their subjects. The most common tests are for medicine and law, usually the BMAT, the UKCAT and the LNAT.

The BioMedical Admissions Test (BMAT): used by six UK and six overseas universities for admission to dentistry, medicine, veterinary science and biomedical sciences.

This is a two-hour pen-and-paper test consisting of the following papers.

- Aptitude and Skills: 35 questions requiring short or multiple-choice answers. This is designed to test problem solving, understanding arguments, data analysis and inference. 60 minutes.
- Scientific Knowledge and Application: 27 questions, again with short or multiple-choice answers. 30 minutes.
- Writing Task: a short essay from a choice of four titles. No prior knowledge is required. You will be expected to develop ideas and explain them effectively. 30 minutes.

You must apply to sit the test by 1 October, or up to 15 October on payment of a penalty fee, and you must sit the test on the one date that is offered in any one year. This is in early November. You may sit the test at your school or college if it is a registered assessment centre or at an 'open centre' (often an independent school that accepts external candidates). There are test centres in many countries.

The cost is £46 (Home and EU students) or £78 (international students), with an additional fee of £32 for late applications. You can get full information, including many more past questions and advice on how to prepare, at www.admissionstesting.org. If you are going to sit the test outside the UK, you should enquire whether the test centre you will attend uses QWERTY, AZERTY or other keyboards.

BMAT® Aptitude & Skills Practice Questions

Have a go at the below sample BMAT Aptitude and Skills practice questions, taken from the full test.

DIRECTIONS (for full test):

Answer every question. Points are awarded for correct answers only. There are no penalties for incorrect answers.

All questions are worth 1 mark.

---

1. To celebrate the countdown to Christmas, a cable network airs the same four Christmas films in the same order, without break or interruption, from 23rd December until just after midnight on 25th December.

The film cycle starts with *A Christmas Story* and ends with *It's a Wonderful Life*; the complete cycle (with running times of each film) was as follows:

A Christmas Story	94 minutes
Home Alone	115 minutes
Elf	97 minutes
It's a Wonderful Life	135 minutes

The films have been scheduled so that the cycle will end when *It's a Wonderful Life* finishes at 12.01am on 25th December.

Which film is the first to play in its entirety on 24th December, and when does it start playing?

A *A Christmas Story* at 1.58am

B *Home Alone* at 1.29am

C *Elf* at 1.40am

D *It's a Wonderful Life* at 1.34am

2. Media coverage of organ donation has increased as the Government considers making the donor registry 'opt-out', rather than 'opt-in'. Every week, newspapers and TV reports are filled with grim stories and statistics of waiting lists and deaths of those waiting for a transplant. Regardless of any changes to legislation, the media could do more to increase organ donation at present. For example, the frequent news reports on the need for more donated organs rarely mention how, exactly, members of the public can 'opt-in' to the donor registry. This practice stands in stark contrast to the presentation of such stories in other countries, such as the USA and Canada, where stories on the need for more organ donors almost always end with contact details for joining the donor registry. Providing viewers with a phone number or website for joining the registry is seen as a public service, part of the media's responsibility in calling attention to such a problem.

Which of the following best summarises the main conclusion of the argument?

A It's easier to become an organ donor in the USA or Canada than in the UK.

B Sometimes the media can help to solve the problems it identifies.

C The Government wants to make organ donation compulsory.

D Many people die waiting for organs each year as there are too few donors opting-in to the registry.

E Everyone should be required to join the organ donor registry.

UK Clinical Aptitude Test (UKCAT): used by 26 UK and three overseas universities for entry to medicine and dentistry

UKCAT is an online test consisting of the following sections.

- Verbal Reasoning: designed to assess ability to think logically about written information and to arrive at a reasoned conclusion. 22 minutes.
- Quantitative Reasoning: assesses ability to solve numerical problems. 25 minutes.
- Abstract Reasoning: assesses ability to infer relationships from information by convergent and divergent thinking. 13 minutes.
- Decision Making: assesses ability to deal with various forms of information, to infer relationships, to make informed judgements, and to decide on an appropriate response to situations given. 32 minutes.
- Situational Judgement: measures capacity to understand real-world situations and to identify critical factors and appropriate behaviour in dealing with them. 27 minutes.

All answers are multiple choice.

The test must be taken online at an approved test centre. There are centres in 88 countries and there are many in the UK, so you should be able to find one within convenient travelling distance.

You may register to take the test from 2 May and there are several test dates between 3 July and 3 October.

The cost varies at different centres: at those in the EU it is £65 if the test is taken in July or August, or £85 in September or October. Outside the EU the cost is £115. If you are going to sit the test outside the UK, you should enquire whether the test centre you will attend uses QWERTY, AZERTY or other keyboards.

If you have any disabilities or additional needs that require you to have extra time in exams, you should make sure to register for the UKCATSEN rather than the regular test. If you need special access arrangements for examinations, you should contact Pearson VUE customer services directly to discuss your personal requirements before booking the test.

Full information, including a guide to what to expect at a test centre, is given at www.ukcat.ac.uk.

Law National Aptitude Test (LNAT): used by eight UK universities for entry to law

LNAT is a two-part online test that takes two and a quarter hours. It is designed to test the skills required to study law, but does not require any previous knowledge.

Section A consists of 42 multiple-choice questions based on argumentative passages. Candidates are given 95 minutes to answer all of the questions. For Section B, candidates have 40 minutes to answer one of five essay questions on a range of subjects and demonstrate their ability to argue economically to a conclusion, displaying a good command of written English.

There is no set date for sitting the test, but you may take it from 1 September. The standard closing date for sitting the test is 20 January, but some universities require results by an earlier date.

Tests are offered at 500 centres around the world, including 150 in the UK. The cost is £50 at EU centres and £70 at those outside the EU. If you are going to sit the LNAT test outside the UK you should enquire whether test centres use QWERTY, AZERTY or other keyboards.

There is much more information on the LNAT website, www.lnat.ac.uk, where you can find out more about the different parts of the test and read some tips on both tackling multiple-choice questions and writing the kind of essay that will impress.

Can you prepare for BMAT, UKCAT and LNAT?

You cannot learn or revise anything for these tests. However, you can certainly prepare for them by finding out what to expect and practising, using practice papers, which are freely available online. You should also familiarise yourself with the type of equipment in the case of computer-based tests.

> **TIP!**
>
> Bursaries are available for all three tests for applicants who would have difficulty in meeting the cost. Full details are on the websites.

Other entrance tests

If you apply to either Oxford or Cambridge you will find that for many courses you will be required to take an additional test. NB as of 2017 entry, Cambridge has introduced common-format written assessments for all subjects except mathematics and music. You can very quickly find a list on the two universities' individual websites.

Many other universities and colleges also use entry tests for particular courses. You can find a full list of those that have been declared to UCAS with details of how and where you can take them, on the UCAS website. The majority of tests are set and administered by the organisation Admissions Testing Service, which is also responsible for BMAT.

The two most common tests are the Sixth Term Examination Paper (STEP) and the Thinking Skills Assessment (TSA).

STEP (Sixth Term Examination Paper)

The test consists of up to three, three-hour, paper-based examinations. Candidates are usually required to sit either one or two of the examinations, depending on the requirements of the universities they have applied to. It is taken at the end of the A level period – normally at your school or college, or otherwise at a test centre. Currently, STEP is used by Cambridge and Warwick universities. Mathematics departments in other universities may ask you to take specific STEP papers. You can check by looking on their websites.

If your school or college does not pay the fee it is £50 per single paper, plus an additional £19 late entry fee.

Thinking Skills Assessment (TSA)

This test is designed to test the sort of skills that are not always covered in school-based exams – such as critical thinking and problem solving. It is a pen-and-paper test consisting of two sections:

Section 1 Multiple-choice questions: 50 questions covering problem solving (numerical and spatial reasoning) and critical thinking (understanding argument and reasoning using everyday language). Usually in multiple-choice format. 90 minutes.

Section 2 Writing Task (not always used): tests ability to organise ideas in a clear and concise manner, and communicate them effectively in writing in a 30-minute essay chosen from four titles (on general topics – not linked to specific subjects).

The test is normally taken on the same day as an interview.

Currently the TSA is used by Cambridge, Oxford and University College, London for some of their courses. The test is free to take, but some test centres may charge a fee to use their service.

Mathematics Admissions Test (MAT)

Some universities prefer to use this pencil-and-paper test produced by the Admissions Testing Service in partnership with the University of Oxford. Current users are Cambridge, Imperial College, London and Oxford. The test takes 2 hours and 30 minutes. The University of Warwick does not insist on the test, but a good score may result in a reduced offer. The test is free to take, but some test centres may charge a fee to use their service

Test of Mathematics for University Admissions

This test is produced by the Admissions Testing Service.

Currently applicants are *encouraged* to take this test by the universities of Durham, Lancaster and Sheffield, which all state that a good score in the test may result in a lower advanced-level offer.

The test is normally taken in schools or colleges, but external test centres are available. The test costs £29 for Home and EU students and £40 for non-EU students, plus an additional £20 late entry fee.

Resources

Publications

- *Getting into* series, Trotman Education, www.trotman.co.uk. The series gives advice on securing a place at university for courses leading to professional careers (e.g. business and economics; dentistry; law; medicine; psychology; veterinary science); and on gaining a place on courses at Oxford and Cambridge.
- *Heap 2019: University Degree Course Offers*, Trotman Education, www.trotman.co.uk.
- *University Interviews*, Trotman Education, www.trotman.co.uk.

Websites

- www.admissionstesting.org (BMAT, MAT, STEP and TSA).
- www.ukcat.ac.uk (UKCAT).
- www.lnat.ac.uk (LNAT).
- www.ucas.com/trackyourapplication.

NB: All the test websites offer free practice tests.

10 | Exam results and afterwards

This chapter looks at what might happen when you have your exam results. However, please don't skip the chapter and think 'I don't need to read this yet!' You might not need any of the information, but then again you might – and panic stations can set in in the summer. A lot of people whose exam results are not what they hoped for make rushed decisions, leaping at the first option that presents itself. They can live to regret doing so.

This chapter discusses what happens at exam results time and the options you might have if you need or decide to change your plans. These include:

- Adjustment
- Clearing
- rethinking your higher education plans, perhaps retaking certain subjects or taking different ones
- deciding not to do a higher education course at all.

Before results day

Most applicants are accepted conditionally before their exam results are known, so the results of exams taken or assessments completed in May/June are very important.

After you have taken your exams, you deserve to relax; but it is worth giving some thought to what you will do if you do not get the grades needed for your higher education place – a sort of 'Plan B'. Will you try to secure a place through Clearing (see page 103)? Would you rather retake and apply again next year for the course you really want to do? Or are you having doubts about whether higher education is really for you?

If you are ill or have some other problem at exam time that you think may adversely affect your results, tell the universities and colleges whose offers you are holding, or ask your school or college to contact them on your behalf. You may need to get a doctor's certificate to support your case. Admissions tutors will do their best to take such circumstances into account, but they must know about them before your results come out. If you leave it until after you have disappointing results, it may be too late.

Results day

YOU WILL NOT SEE YOUR RESULTS IN TRACK. Your school, college or exam board will give them to you.

IB results are usually issued in the first week in July. Unless you plan to go to your school or college in person you will need to access them online. To do this you will need your PIN and personal code that your IB programme coordinator will have given you earlier in the year. Remember to find out what time your results are released, as this is done at different times in different time zones; usually the UK receives them around 2pm.

SQA results will be released on 7 August 2018. Clearing vacancies will be available on www.ucas.com from the beginning of July. Your results will be sent to you to arrive in the post on results day. If you have signed up to MySQA and activated your account by 20 July you may request to have these sent via email or text.

A level results will be published on Thursday 15 August. Adjustment will start the same day. You should be able to find out from Track from the morning onwards whether your place has been confirmed. But you won't see your results. You will have to contact your school or college for them – usually by going in at a time you have been given. If admissions tutors are still considering whether to give you a place Track won't be updated yet. BUT remember that if you meet or exceed the exact terms of your offer your place is guaranteed. It is only people who have not done so who may need to wait.

UCAS receives most results from the exam boards and, after checking that they match the information on your application, sends them to the universities and colleges where you are holding any offers of a place. You can check at www.ucas.com/sending-exam-results to see the full list of qualifications for which UCAS will do this.

If yours isn't listed it means you will have to send your results to your universities or colleges yourself. If you have taken any other exams, such as Nationals 4 and 5, GCSE or international qualifications, you must send your results as soon as you receive them to those universities and colleges where you are holding offers. (IB results may or may not be received by UCAS as schools and colleges need to give permission for this.)

When your results are released and have been received by the admissions tutors, they will compare your results with the conditions they set and make a decision on whether to accept you.

What if you get the grades?

Congratulations! Your place will be confirmed; a university or college cannot reject you if you have met the conditions of your offer. Before the end of August, you'll see in Track that your place is confirmed; check your online confirmation letter to see if you need to take any further action to confirm your place.

> **TIP!**
>
> Arrange your holidays so you are at home when the results are published. Even if all goes well and your grades are acceptable, you may need to confirm your place and deal with your registration, accommodation and loan. And, if things haven't gone according to plan, you need to take advice, find out about course vacancies and make some quick decisions about possible offers in the Clearing system.

Adjustment

Adjustment might give you an opportunity to reconsider where and what to study.

If you met all the conditions of your firm choice and **exceeded at least one** you could change your place for one on another course you may now prefer. Adjustment begins on A level results day and lasts until 31 August. If you register but do not find an alternative course, you keep your place at your original firm-choice institution.

Only a small number of applicants receive places through Adjustment. In 2017 the total was 1,040.

How Adjustment works

For you to be eligible to use Adjustment:

- your results must have met and exceeded the conditions of your conditional firm choice
- you need to have paid the full application fee (£24 for two to five choices).

You are not eligible to use Adjustment if:

- you are confirmed at your firm choice but did not exceed the conditions of the offer
- your results have met and exceeded the conditions of your conditional insurance choice
- you have a confirmed place on a changed course offer
- your original offer was unconditional.

To use Adjustment you will need to:

- register in Track by clicking on 'Find out about and register for adjustment' on the 'Your choices' screen
- contact a university or college to find another place. You will have five 24-hour periods (including weekends) within this time to use it, starting from when your conditional firm offer changes to unconditional firm (UF), or on A results day – whichever is the later. If your offer goes UF less than five days before 31 August, you'll only have whatever time is left between then and 31 August.

The university or college will check that you met and exceeded the conditions of your firm choice and will tell you if they can offer you a place. You tell them if you want to accept it.

If you are accepted through Adjustment, Track will be updated with the new choice and you'll find a new confirmation letter available for you to print.

Case study

Jessica Boyce from Hertfordshire is in her third year of a Law degree at Newcastle University. This is not the course she originally chose. She got into Newcastle through Adjustment.

She was holding an offer from the University of Leeds to study International Relations, with the intention of taking a postgraduate conversion course for Law. During the course of her second year of A levels she changed her mind and decided that she would rather do a Law degree. Despite excellent grades of A*, A and B in Politics, History and English she was unable to do a straightforward course change at Leeds.

'I rang as soon as I got my results but they were unable to help because all their applicants to Law had met their offers and there were no places left. However, I had exceeded the terms of my own offer – AAB – and so I knew that I was eligible for Adjustment.

'I decided to see what might be available. Manchester and Newcastle were both offering places. I rang both and both said they would take me. I then had to decide. I looked them up on the UCAS website but what clinched it for me was that I already knew something about Newcastle because my sister had applied there the previous year (although she went somewhere else).

'Under Adjustment rules I didn't have much time. I spent a day thinking it over and talked to my director of studies, my family and a family friend who is a solicitor.

'When I had decided what to do I rang Newcastle to accept the place and was told that I had first to get Leeds to release me. This was not a problem and the emails came through from UCAS immediately to show me that my place at Leeds had been cancelled and that I had a confirmed offer from Newcastle.

'All I had to do then was arrange accommodation. The students who had made Newcastle their firm choice had had priority but I was ahead of people coming through Clearing. I was offered a place in hall with no difficulty but it was further away from the campus than I wanted. Luckily, I was able to organise an exchange and get a room in a hall I did like!'

TIP!

You can check universities' and colleges' decisions on results day via Track.

If you missed out ...

Do not panic! You should contact admissions offices immediately to find out whether they will accept you anyway. This is because admissions tutors may decide to confirm your offer even if you failed to meet some of the conditions. It has been known for applicants to be accepted with much lower grades if there are places available, there is good school or college support and, perhaps, a good interview record, although this varies greatly from course to course. But don't count on this! Alternatively, you may be offered a place on a different course.

UCAS will send you an official notification of the outcome of your application. If you have been offered a place on an alternative course, you will have a choice of actions. These will be listed in the notification letter.

If your place is not confirmed, you can find a place through Clearing (see below) or, alternatively, you can retake your exams and apply again the following year.

Clearing

If you do not get the grades you had hoped for and your offer is not confirmed, don't worry. If you're flexible and you have reasonable exam results, there is still a good chance you could find another course through Clearing, which helps those without a place to find one. In 2017, 66,865 students found places by using this service, an increase of 3.1% on the previous year (1,990 more acceptances).

You are eligible for Clearing if you paid the full application fee and you have not withdrawn from the UCAS system and:

- you are not holding any offers (either because you did not receive any, or because you declined the offers you did receive)

or
- your offers have not been confirmed because you have not met the conditions (such as not achieving the required grades)

or
- you made your UCAS application too late for it to be considered in the normal way (after 30 June).

What do I have to do?

You need to search the lists of courses with vacancies to see if there are any that interest you. Course vacancies are published from the beginning of July until late September. Arrangements for the publication of vacancies vary from year to year and precise sources of guidance for the summer of 2019 will be announced by UCAS closer to the time. Usually, official lists of vacancies are published in the UCAS search tool and in some national newspapers. The national Exam Results Helpline on 0808 100 8000, which is staffed by trained advisers, is also a useful source of information and advice. You will also see many advertisements for universities and colleges with vacant places in the national press.

Make a list of the courses that interest you and contact the institutions, in order of your preference, to ask whether they will accept you. It is recommended that you telephone, email or call in person because the admissions tutor will want to speak to you personally, not to your parent or teacher. Keep your Clearing number (given in Track) to hand as you will probably be asked for it. If you're not convinced that a course is right for you, remember that you do not have to commit yourself. You need to contact universities or colleges direct about any vacancies you are interested in.

If one agrees to give you a place on the course you want, you enter the institution and course details in UCAS Track and they will then be able to accept you. Only when you are certain you have found the right course should you accept an offer of a place. When you have accepted you will not be able to take any further part in Clearing and you will be committed to taking up your place. Figure 2 on the next page gives tips on what you might do if you do not get a place through Clearing.

Top tips on Clearing

- Talk to your careers adviser about which courses and subjects would be most suitable for you, particularly if your original UCAS application was unsuccessful.
- Remember that you can apply for any course that has places left – you do not need to keep to the same subjects for which you first applied. If you do decide to apply for courses that are quite different from the ones you originally selected, make sure you do your

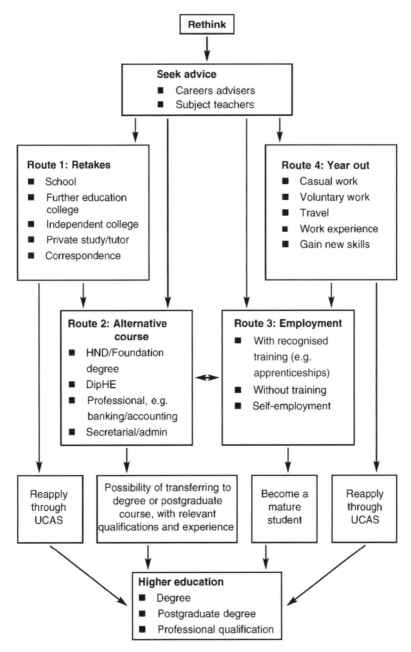

Figure 2: Alternatives to going to university in 2019

research very thoroughly, referring back to prospectuses and websites. Remember, though, that you will not be able to change your personal statement.

- Although you will have to act quickly, do not make any hasty decisions; accept an offer only if you are sure the course is right for you.

- One way of making sure you are happy with your choice of course is to go to the university or college in person: the best way to find out more is to pay it a visit. Most universities and colleges are happy to make arrangements to meet applicants and show them around, and many will have Clearing open days. They know that you could be spending the next three or four years there, and will be reassured that you want to be sure you are making the right choice.
- If you are applying for art and design courses, you may need to supply a portfolio of work as well as your Clearing number.
- Remember that universities and colleges are likely to refer back to your UCAS application when deciding whether to make you an offer. So, it is a good idea to have another look at what you wrote on your personal statement to make sure you are familiar with it, just in case an admissions tutor wants to ask you about it.

Why do you have to wait until August for Adjustment and for some Clearing vacancies?

After all, some people know their results earlier in the year – in June for example. The reason is that both services operate to fill empty places in universities and colleges. They do not know how many of these they have until the last of the major exam results – A levels – are known. Only then, when they know how many applicants have qualified for places and have firmly accepted them, do they know what they have left. Some admissions staff may not put their places into Clearing immediately. They might wait until they see how many students apply through Adjustment – or even as completely new applicants – before they decide to give places to less well-qualified applicants through Clearing.

When you have secured a place through Adjustment or Clearing

Make sure you get from your new choice of university or college the information you will need about:

- accommodation
- term dates
- introductory arrangements.

Retakes

Remember, disappointing results need not mean the end of your ambitions. If low grades mean that you have not been accepted on a course of your choice, you could consider retaking your exams or changing to a new subject if you think that would give you a better chance of improving your grades.

- Retakes of A levels and Scottish Highers are available only once each year – in June.
- IB retakes are available in both November and May. There are some restrictions so you will need to contact the centre where you might want to do your retakes.

While most university and college departments consider retake candidates – and some welcome the greater maturity and commitment to hard work that retaking demonstrates – be aware that you may be asked for higher grades. It is always worth checking with the relevant admissions tutor that your proposed retake programme is acceptable. It is very rare for Oxford or Cambridge to accept applicants who have retaken their exams, for example.

Part III

Using Apply to submit your UCAS application

11 | Introducing Apply

Apply is UCAS's online application system. It is found at www.ucas.com/apply. As well as being easy and convenient to use, it:

- speeds up the processing of applications to higher education courses
- incorporates checks that prevent you from making simple errors
- is supported by the very latest UCAS course data and relevant additional information.

This chapter provides a brief outline of the Apply process, giving you guidelines on setting up your account, together with tips for making the application process as easy as possible. The remaining chapters of this book work through each section of the online application.

Getting started

Using Apply via a school or college

Each June, all schools, colleges and careers centres registered with UCAS can access the Apply application system and set it up for the coming application cycle. Your UCAS coordinator will set up a unique password or 'buzzword', made up of at least six letters and numerals, which will be used by you and all other UCAS applicants at your centre so that your application can be identified with that centre.

TIP!

The buzzword allows you to log in to Apply and lets UCAS see which centre you are from. When you enter your buzzword, do not hit the return key. Use the 'Next' button or the buzzword will not be accepted.

You can access the Apply system from any computer on the internet. The first thing you have to do is register. As you move through the registration screens, you will be asked to provide personal details including your first name(s), surname, title, gender, date of birth, address, telephone number(s) and email address, and agree to the UCAS terms and conditions.

Apply will check your details with you (they will automatically be entered into the personal details section of your application, where you will have the opportunity to change them later). You will be asked to choose a unique password and select four security questions with answers. When you have completed the registration section your username will appear on screen. Keep a note of this and your password as you can use these details to log in and use Apply at any time and in any place where there is access to the internet, from Thailand to Tyneside. After you have registered, the first time you log in to use Apply you will be asked if you are applying through a centre or as an individual. If you indicate that you are applying through your school or college, you will be asked to enter its buzzword. After you have added your school or college details, your Personal ID will appear on screen – make a note of this as you will need it in future communications with UCAS and with universities and colleges.

Using Apply as an individual

If you want to apply to study on a higher education course but are not attached to a school or college, you can – quite easily from anywhere with internet access – make an application using Apply.

To start, click 'Register' on the UCAS website home page (www.ucas.com) and select the appropriate link. When you have read through the guidance, click the 'register and apply' link. You will be asked to choose a password and four security questions and answers. When you have completed the registration section, you will be issued – on screen – with a username that you must note down and keep secure.

After you have registered, the first time you log in to use Apply you will be asked if you are applying through a centre or as an individual. You should choose 'individual'.

> **TIP!**
>
> If you forget your username or password you can use the 'Forgotten login?' service on the Apply login page. Enter the email address you used in your application and UCAS will send you a reminder of your username and a link to reset your password.

You will be asked to answer a set of straightforward eligibility questions to start your application. Your Personal ID will then be displayed on screen – make a note of this as you will need it in future communications with UCAS and with universities and colleges.

After this, the only difference between making an application as an individual and making it via a school, college or other UCAS-registered centre is the procedure for providing a reference (see below). You may apply as an individual and ask your old school to supply your reference if you have left recently. To do this, click on 'Options' in the left-hand menu and click on 'Ask a registered school, college or organisation to write your reference only'; you will need to supply the buzzword. When they have added the reference they will return your application to you to forward to UCAS.

Reference

If you are applying through a UCAS-registered centre, you complete all the sections of your application and then give or send it to your referee to add the reference; the referee is likely to be one of your teachers, personal tutor or head of sixth form. If you are applying as an individual with an independent referee, you enter your referee's details in the reference section of your application and then Apply will send him or her an automated email to ask for a reference. UCAS then sends your referee a username and password to enter a reference directly onto your application through a secure website. Your reference must be written by a responsible person who knows you well enough to comment on your suitability for the courses you have applied to. This could be an employer, a senior colleague in employment or voluntary work, a trainer, a careers adviser or the teacher of a relevant further education course you have recently attended. Your referee cannot be a member of your family, a friend, partner or ex-partner.

Because individuals' UCAS applications are sent direct to UCAS after a reference has been provided (rather than to a referee at school or college to forward), it is a good idea to use the 'View all details' function to view your form and print out a copy to keep before submitting it to UCAS.

If you have any difficulties at any stage, there is help in Apply and on the UCAS website, or you can contact the UCAS Customer Experience Centre on 0371 468 0 468 between 08.30 and 18.00 hours (UK time) on weekdays.

> **TIP!**
>
> Make sure that you allow plenty of time for the person writing your reference to complete it before the UCAS application deadline. They may receive several requests at the same time. If you are a student at a school or college you will probably be given an internal deadline.

Technical requirements

The UCAS application systems are designed to be accessed via an internet-connected computer. They may work on other devices, but their functionality would be unsupported by UCAS.

Browser

To be able to use Apply, you will need access to a suitable web browser. UCAS supports its online application systems on the following browsers:

- Internet Explorer (version 9 or higher)
- Google Chrome (latest version)
- Firefox (latest version)
- Safari (on Mac, latest version).

The systems may work on other browsers, but, again, their functionality would be unsupported by UCAS. It's recommended that you use a recent version of your chosen browser as older versions may be less secure.

Most web browsers allow you to 'cache' the web pages you view. This means that they will be temporarily stored on your computer. However, in some instances, caching web pages will not allow you to update your data in Apply. To avoid this, select the browser setting that ensures that pages are reloaded every time you view them.

The method of selecting caching options varies from browser to browser. For example, on Internet Explorer:

- choose 'Tools' from the toolbar at the top of the browser
- from the subsequent menu, select 'Internet options'
- click on the 'Settings' button under 'Temporary internet files'
- under the heading 'Check for newer versions of stored pages', choose 'Every visit to the page'.

Your browser must also:

- have 128-bit encryption enabled
- have JavaScript enabled.

Your computer set-up also needs to comply with the following.

- Your monitor should be at least 15 inches in size.
- Your display should be set to at least 256 colours.
- Your screen should be set to a resolution of 800 × 600 or above.

If you are unsure about any of these points, consult your computer manual or help facility.

Navigating Apply

On the registration screen, you can select English or Welsh from a drop-down list.

In Apply you can choose to receive correspondence from course providers and from UCAS in Welsh. After that, you can use the 'Options/Opsiynau' link in the left-hand navigation bar at any time to change the language.

The help text in Apply is available in Welsh too.

It is not possible to apply in any language other than English or Welsh.

When you log in, you will be taken to the main Apply screen. Apply is divided into the following sections:

- personal details
- additional information
- student finance
- choices
- education
- employment
- statement
- reference
- view all details
- pay/send.

You can access each section by clicking on its name to the left of the screen. There are on-screen instructions in every section, guiding you through what you have to do. If you get stuck at any point, you can access help text by clicking on the 'Help' button or on the question mark next to each section. The text relates directly to the task you are completing at that point. Figure 3 on the next page shows what the 'Welcome' screen looks like.

Some screens in Apply have 'Next' and 'Previous' buttons allowing you to move from page to page. You must use these because the back and forward buttons on your web browser will not be visible.

Every now and then, you may be presented with an error screen telling you that the page hasn't been found and suggesting that you click 'Refresh'. Do not panic; just right-click on the screen and select 'Refresh'. The page should then be restored and you can continue as normal.

You are free to move between sections as you like, leaving them partially completed ('In progress') and returning to them later if necessary. When you've completed a section, just tick the 'Section completed' box and then click on 'Save'. Any inaccurate or missing information will be highlighted in green to indicate that it is not yet complete. If this section is completed correctly, a red tick will appear. Even if you confirm that the section is finished, you can still return to it and update it or add extra information if you need to.

Checking the progress of your application

The status of your application is displayed on the left of the screen. It shows whether each section of Apply is 'Not started', 'In progress' or 'Completed'. A red tick next to a section shows that the section is completed.

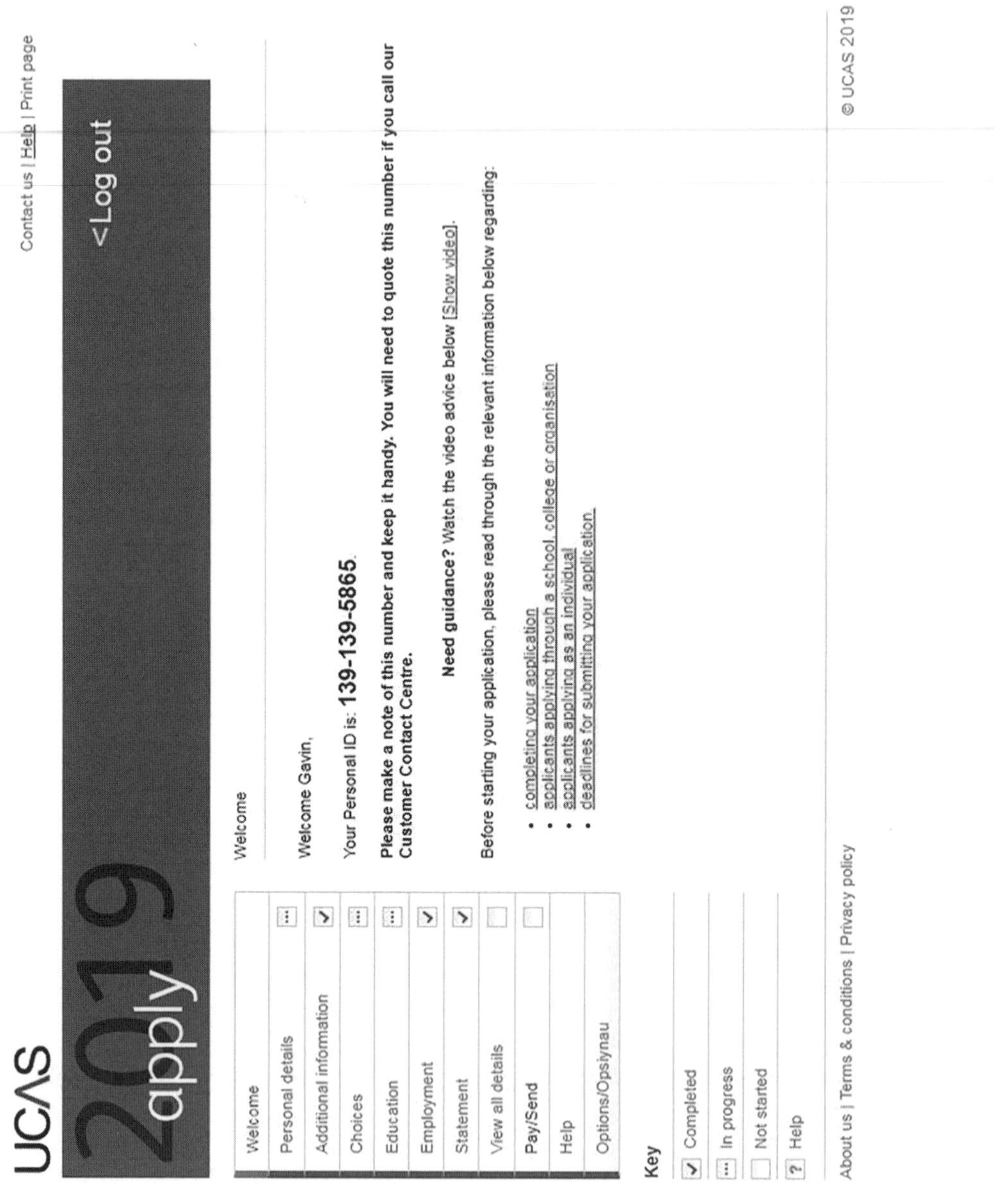

UCAS
2019
apply

Contact us | Help | Print page

<Log out

Welcome	
Personal details	⋮
Additional information	✓
Choices	⋮
Education	⋮
Employment	✓
Statement	✓
View all details	☐
Pay/Send	☐
Help	
Options/Opsiynau	

Key

✓	Completed
⋮	In progress
☐	Not started
?	Help

Welcome

Welcome Gavin,

Your Personal ID is: **139-139-5865**.

Please make a note of this number and keep it handy. You will need to quote this number if you call our Customer Contact Centre.

Need guidance? Watch the video advice below [Show video].

Before starting your application, please read through the relevant information below regarding:

- completing your application
- applicants applying through a school, college or organisation
- applicants applying as an individual
- deadlines for submitting your application

About us | Terms & conditions | Privacy policy

© UCAS 2019

Figure 3: Welcome screen

At any stage while you're using Apply, you can click on 'View all details' to preview or print a copy of your application in a viewer-friendly format. This will enable you to check through what you've done quickly and easily. Any incomplete sections will be highlighted in green.

> **TIP!**
>
> Remember to save all your changes.

You will not be able to submit your application until every section of Apply is complete. Once you have finished your application, agreed to the UCAS declaration and sent it to your referee or asked UCAS to contact your referee, the status of your application will appear every time you log in, at one of the following stages:

- Application not checked
- Application checked
- Reference not yet started
- Reference in progress
- Reference awaiting approval
- Application sent to UCAS
- Your Personal ID is....

Once you have submitted your application to UCAS and received your welcome email, you can use Track to keep up-to-date with your progress and reply to your offers.

Security tips

For data protection reasons, Apply is a secure area of the UCAS website. More recent web browsers have a built-in feature allowing you to save your password so that you do not have to remember or retype it later. However, if you use this facility it will allow anyone using that particular computer to log in to your account and change the details of your application. For this reason, it is strongly advised that you do not use this feature.

When you have finished a session using Apply, it is strongly recommended that you log out properly by using the 'Log out' button (not by simply closing the window you are in). Once you have logged out you should close your web browser down completely. This will ensure that no one will be able to access your details.

How the rest of this book works

The remaining chapters of this book will take you step-by-step through each section of Apply, giving you general advice on the nature of the information you are asked for and the basic principles of getting it right. Each area of Apply has a corresponding chapter in this book.

- **Personal details**: basic facts such as name, address and date of birth.
- **Additional information** (for UK applicants only): mostly data for equal opportunities monitoring.
- **Choices**: your selection of universities, colleges and subjects.
- **Education**: your school or college details and exams, past and future.
- **Employment**: any jobs you have held.
- **Personal statement**: the most important section.

In each chapter, the subheadings relate directly to the headings used in Apply, so you can easily locate the relevant information.

The final part of the book deals with finishing off your application, including information on:

- your declaration: your agreement with UCAS and higher education institutions
- submitting your application
- fee payment
- your reference.

At the end of the book you will find a chapter on troubleshooting (Chapter 19), which will help you solve some of the most frequently encountered problems. Further help is available via the 'Help' text accessible on individual Apply screens.

Stop and think!

Before you start your application, here are some final tips and reminders.

- Make sure you have done all your research thoroughly and you are happy with your choices. If in doubt, take another look at Part I of this book, 'In the think tank'.
- Collect together:
  - your personal details
  - all school or college attendance dates
  - exam results slips and entry forms
  - any employment details

    o   details of the higher education courses you are applying for, including institution and course codes (you can find these on the search tool on the UCAS website).

- Carefully read through the guidance available on the Apply home page.
- Be honest and truthful – you must be able to back up all your statements.
- Do not try to make more than one application in the same year.
- Remember that once your application reaches UCAS, you cannot amend it or add anything to it.

You should now be ready to start your application – read on, and good luck!

12| Personal details

Obviously, UCAS and the universities and colleges to which you are applying need to know who you are and where they can get hold of you. There is little use in applying if they do not! What is less obvious is that they will need to know about a number of other aspects of your life. This can be for important financial reasons (e.g. in deciding who assesses your eligibility for funding) or to determine whether you require any additional support while studying, for example if you have a disability. Your application will therefore contain quite a lot of information about you, which we will deal with here.

You may already have entered some of it when you registered for Apply – this information will have been transferred into the personal details section of the application, where you can amend it.

Specifically, this section covers the following:

- personal information:
    - name, gender and address
    - preferred first name
    - telephone numbers, email address and date of birth
    - residential category and nationality
- Unique Learner Number
- student support:
    - fee code
    - student support arrangements
- mailings from UCAS
- nominated access
- criminal convictions
- disability/special needs
- Test of English as a Foreign Language (TOEFL) number
- International English Language Testing System (IELTS) number.

Personal information

The information you entered when you registered will have been drawn through into the details part of your application. You can edit or alter it at this stage.

Name, gender and address

You are asked to enter your name 'exactly as it is stated on official documents, such as your passport, birth certificate or driving licence'. Whatever you give as your title, name and address will form the basis of your UCAS and university or college record. Although it may sound surprising, every year there are a number of applicants who make elementary errors when entering their own names! The following example is fine:

- Title: Ms
- Surname/family name: Jones
- First/given name(s): Rachel.

The example below, however, will cause problems (and a lot of people do this):

- Title: Mr
- Surname/family name: Robarts
- First/given name(s): Mark Robarts.

Sorry, Mark – but for ever afterwards, you will be Mr M R Robarts to UCAS and the universities and colleges to which you are applying. This will mean that your name will not match your exam certificates, passport, etc., so take care when entering your details. If your name is not easily divided into surname and first names, decide how you want to be addressed and stick to it.

For example:

- Title: Mr
- Surname/family name: Hassan
- First/given name(s): Nik Kamal.

Chinese students, whose own custom is to put the family name first, will normally have to accept being addressed in the Western style – so the following example will appear as C H A Wong:

- Title: Ms
- Surname/family name: Wong
- First/given name(s): Chu-Hai Angela.

It is just possible that universities and colleges may address you as Wong Chu-Hai, but do not count on it. If you have adopted a Western name, feel free to include it.

Preferred first name

If you have a different name you would rather be known as, please enter it in this field. For example, your proper first name is Andrew but you are known as Andy.

> **TIP!**
>
> Do not provide nicknames. It is important that you enter the same names that appear on official documents such as exam certificates.

Gender

For gender, you are asked to choose either male or female.

Address

The address section should not present you with any particularly challenging problems. Your postal address is the one that will appear in the UCAS record, and is where written correspondence about your application will be sent. This does not have to be your home address; you are at liberty to have your letters sent anywhere you choose – your school, for example.

If you do decide to give your school address, you will need to change your address to your home address, or another more suitable location, once you leave school – UCAS will not do this automatically. You can do this yourself online using Track. (Tell your university or college as well.) If you do not inform UCAS, offers of places or details of Clearing opportunities will be sent to your school. This will mean a delay in you receiving them and you could lose a place as a result.

Telephone numbers, email address and date of birth

An email address is compulsory. It will be used by UCAS to contact you throughout the application process, so make sure you give one that you use regularly. You can also include your home telephone number and mobile number. Some admissions tutors prefer to communicate electronically, and it can speed up communication dramatically at Confirmation and Clearing time.

Make sure you include the area code in your home number, but do not use brackets, spaces, dashes or the '+' symbol. If it is an overseas number, remember to include the international dialling code.

Your date of birth is required for UCAS' and institutions' records: select the day, month and year from the drop-down lists.

Residential category and nationality

Indicating whether your permanent home is in the UK or elsewhere should be straightforward, but your area of permanent residence is less so. If you live:

- outside the UK: name the country (e.g. Australia)
- in Scotland: name the district or islands area (e.g. Clackmannan-shire)
- in Greater London: name the London borough (e.g. Bexley)
- in a former metropolitan district: name the district (e.g. Sefton)
- elsewhere in the UK: name the county (e.g. Northamptonshire).

Apply provides a pop-up list of counties and boroughs for you to choose from if you answered 'Yes' to 'Is your permanent home in the UK?', and a list of countries if you answered 'No'.

Your country of birth and nationality should present no problems, although it is worth mentioning that if you were born in the UK, you should select 'United Kingdom' for the former and 'UK national' for the latter (i.e. you cannot select 'Scotland', 'English', etc.). This information is for statistical purposes only, to find out where applicants come from. It will not be used for selection purposes.

If your country of birth is not in the UK, you will also have to indicate your date of first entry to live in the UK. Using the drop-down lists, you should enter the date when you entered, or propose to enter, the UK.

Residential category can be more complicated, but it is particularly important because what you enter here will be the point from which universities and colleges will start to classify you as 'home' or 'overseas' for the purpose of tuition fees. Those classified as overseas students pay a much higher annual tuition fee. (Your tuition fee status has no direct connection with your nationality: it depends on your place of ordinary residence and the length of time you have been ordinarily resident there.) You must choose from a list of residential category options (as defined by UCAS), summarised below.

TIP!

If you cannot find your area on the list, you need to look through the existing options to find one that matches your circumstances.

UK citizen – England

You are a UK citizen, or are the child or grandchild, or the spouse or civil partner of a UK citizen, and have lived in England for the past three years, but not just for full-time education. If you have been living in England for three years partly for full-time education, you also lived in England prior to that three-year period.

UK citizen – Scotland

You are a UK citizen, or are the child or grandchild, or the spouse or civil partner of a UK citizen, and have lived in Scotland for the past three years, but not just for full-time education. If you have been living in Scotland for three years partly for full-time education, you also lived in Scotland prior to that three-year period.

UK citizen – Wales

You are a UK citizen, or are the child or grandchild, or the spouse or civil partner of a UK citizen, and have lived in Wales for the past three years, but not just for full-time education. If you have been living in Wales for three years partly for full-time education, you also lived in Wales prior to that three-year period.

UK citizen – Northern Ireland

You are a UK citizen, or are the child or grandchild, or the spouse or civil partner of a UK citizen, and have lived in Northern Ireland for the past three years, but not just for full-time education. If you have been living in Northern Ireland for three years partly for full-time education, you also lived in Northern Ireland prior to that three-year period.

British citizen – Channel Islands and Isle of Man

You are a British citizen, or are the child or grandchild, or the spouse or civil partner of a British citizen, and have lived in the Channel Islands or Isle of Man for the past three years, but not just for full-time education. If you have been living in the Channel Islands or Isle of Man for three years partly for full-time education, you also lived in the Channel Islands or Isle of Man prior to that three-year period.

British citizen – British Overseas Territories

You are a British citizen, or are the child or grandchild, or the spouse or civil partner of a British citizen, and have lived in the British Overseas Territories for the past three years, but not just for full-time education. If you have been living in the British Overseas Territories for three years partly for full-time education, you also lived in the British Overseas Territories prior to that three-year period.

EU national (non-UK citizen)

You are an EU national but not a UK citizen, or are the child or grandchild, or the spouse or civil partner of an EU national (but not a UK citizen), and have lived in the European Economic Area (EEA) or Switzerland or European Overseas Territories (OT) for the past three years, but not just for full-time education. If you have been living in the EEA or Switzerland or OT for three years partly for full-time education, you also lived in the EEA or Switzerland or OT prior to that three-year period.

EEA or Swiss national

Either: You are an EEA or Swiss national working in the UK, or you are the child, spouse or civil partner of such a person or you are the parent or grandparent of an EEA national working in the UK. You have lived in the EEA or Switzerland or OT for the past three years, but not just for full-time education. If you have been living in the EEA, Switzerland or OT for three years partly for full-time education, you also lived in the EEA, Switzerland or OT prior to that three-year period.

Or: You are the child of a Swiss national and have lived in the EEA or Switzerland or OT for the past three years, but not just for full-time education. If you have been living in the EEA, Switzerland or OT for three years partly for full-time education, you also lived in the EEA, Switzerland or OT prior to that three-year period.

Child of a Turkish worker

You are the child of a Turkish national who has lawfully worked in the UK, and you have lived in the EEA, Switzerland or Turkey for the past three years.

Refugee

You have been recognised as a refugee by the British government or you are the spouse, civil partner or child under 18 of such a person at the time of the asylum application.

Humanitarian Protection or similar

You have been granted Exceptional Leave to Enter or Remain, Humanitarian Protection or Discretionary Leave or you are the spouse, civil partner or child under 18 of such a person at the time of the asylum application.

Settled in the UK

You have Indefinite Leave to Enter or Remain in the UK or have the Right of Abode in the UK and have lived in the UK, the Channel Islands or the Isle of Man (or more than one of these) for three years, but not just for full-time education. (However, this does not apply if you are exempt from immigration control, for example, as a diplomat, a member of visiting armed forces or an employee of an international organisation or the family or staff member of such a person; if this is your situation your residential category is Other.)

Other

If you don't fit any of the above categories then answer 'Other'.

Universities and colleges will try to be fair to you, but they do have a duty to apply the regulations equitably to all their students. You could, before applying, write to universities and colleges outlining your circumstances. Some overseas companies have standard letters for employees to use. It sometimes happens that different universities and colleges will classify the same student in different ways, depending on their reading of the rules.

Unique Learner Number (ULN)

You may have a ULN if you started studying for a UK qualification from 2008 onwards. If you have, enter it in the box provided. The ULN should be 10 digits long (i.e. only numbers).

Student support

Use the drop-down list next to 'Fee code' to select which code applies to you. The list below will help you decide which code to choose.

1	Entire cost of tuition fees paid by private finance.
2	Applying for student support assessment by local authority, Student Finance England, Student Finance Wales, SAAS or Student Finance Northern Ireland, Student Loans Company EU Team, Channel Islands or Isle of Man agency.
4	Contribution from a research council.
5	Contribution from the Department of Health or a regional health authority.
6	International student award from the UK government or the British Council.
7	Contribution from a training agency.
8	Contribution from another government source.
9	Contribution from an international agency, government, university or industry.
10	Contribution from UK industry or commerce.
90	Other source of finance.
99	Not known.

Most applicants from the UK, Channel Islands, Isle of Man and the EU will be in category 02. You should use that code if you are eligible for assessment under student support arrangements even if you think your family income will be too high for you to receive support.

If you select fee code 02, there is space provided in the application (under 'Student support arrangements') for you to enter which body will assess your eligibility for funds.

If you are applying for sponsorship, give the name of your first-choice sponsor in the personal statement section. You can find out more about company sponsorship from a careers adviser. You should note in the personal statement (see Chapter 17) if you plan to defer to 2019, should your application for sponsorship this year be unsuccessful. For more information on funding and other financial concerns, see Chapter 3.

Mailings from UCAS

From time to time UCAS sends out information not directly related to your application but covering areas of interest such as funding, sponsorship opportunities, health issues, career possibilities relevant to your chosen subjects and offers of goods or services (such as student banking and travel discounts) relevant to higher education.

Please note that at no time are details of individual applicants released to any of the companies wishing to have information passed to you. Such information may be sent by email, text message or post. You should tick the relevant boxes if you wish or do not wish to receive these mailings.

Direct contact service

This is an optional service you can sign up to. If you find yourself without a place, universities and colleges that you may not have applied to can contact you if they think they have places on courses which might be suitable for you.

Nominated access

You have the option of naming one person who can act on your behalf regarding your application. It is a good idea to do so, in case of illness or injury, for example. You need to fill in their name and their relationship to you.

Criminal convictions

You only need to complete this section if you have a criminal conviction that is **not spent**.

To help the universities and colleges reduce the risk of harm or injury to their students caused by the criminal behaviour of other students, they must know whether an applicant holds any unspent relevant criminal convictions. This information must be entered in the criminal convictions section of the personal details area.

Relevant criminal convictions are convictions for offences against the person, whether of a violent or sexual nature, and convictions for offences involving unlawfully supplying controlled drugs or substances where the conviction concerns commercial drug dealing or trafficking. Convictions that are spent (as defined by the Rehabilitation of Offenders Act 1974) are not considered to be relevant for most courses (see below), and you should not reveal them.

You must tick the box, however, if either of the following statements applies to you.

- I have a relevant criminal conviction that is not spent.
- I am serving a prison sentence for a relevant criminal conviction.

You do not need to include convictions, cautions, warnings or reprimands which are deemed 'protected' under the Rehabilitation of Offenders Act 1974 (Exceptions) Order 1975 (as amended in 2013). Guidance and criteria on the filtering of these cautions and convictions can be found on the Disclosure and Barring Service (DBS) website at: www.gov.uk/government/collections/dbs-filtering-guidance.

(If you are currently serving a prison sentence for a relevant criminal conviction, you must also give the prison address as your postal address on your application and a senior prison officer must support your application.)

If you tick the box, you will not be automatically excluded from the application process; however, the university or college concerned may want to consider the application further or ask for more information before making a decision.

You should be aware that courses in teaching, medicine, dentistry, health, social work, veterinary medicine and veterinary science and courses involving work with children or vulnerable adults, including elderly or sick people, are exempt from the Rehabilitation of Offenders Act 1974 and different rules apply with regard to criminal convictions. For these courses the following points apply.

- The university or college may ask you to agree to a DBS check and, if they do so, you must comply.
- The university or college will send you the appropriate document to fill in. Where this document comes from will depend on the location of the college or university you are applying to.
- The information that will be revealed by the DBS check will vary depending on the type of check required. However, it is likely that, for these courses, the university or college will require either a 'standard' or an 'enhanced' DBS check and either of these checks will reveal spent convictions as well as unspent convictions, cautions (including oral cautions), reprimands, final warnings and binding over orders, irrespective of when these occurred.

- This means that if you have a criminal conviction, spent or unspent, this information will be made known to the university or college (but not UCAS) as part of the DBS check.
- If the DBS check reveals that you have had a conviction, caution, reprimand, final warning or binding over order, the university or college will need to assess your fitness to practise in the profession to which you are applying. Applicants to medicine, for instance, need to be aware that the General Medical Council will not permit students deemed unfit to practise to be entered on the Medical Register, which means that they will not be able to practise as doctors. Similar restrictions might be imposed by other professional bodies, such as, but not limited to, those connected with accountancy, banking, law, social work, teaching and the armed forces.
- You may also be subject to further DBS checks (before and/or after you complete your course) by any prospective employers, who will make their own assessments regarding your fitness to practise in the relevant profession.
- If these issues are in any way relevant to you, you should obtain further advice from appropriate bodies. UCAS will not be able to assist you in this respect.
- You might also be asked to cooperate with other checks that come into force in England, Wales or Northern Ireland at any time during the application process or later. If you are taking a course in Scotland, you will need to comply with any requirements of the Protecting Vulnerable Groups (PVG) scheme that may come into force through Scottish government legislation.

You might find these websites useful:

- www.gov.uk/government/organisations/disclosure-and-barring-service: criminal records check in England and Wales.
- www.justice-ni.gov.uk: criminal records check in Northern Ireland.
- www.mygov.scot/basic-disclosure/apply-for-basic-disclosure: criminal records check in Scotland.

If you are convicted of a relevant criminal offence after you have applied, you must tell both UCAS and any university or college to which you have applied. Do not send details of the offence; simply tell UCAS and the universities or colleges that you have a relevant criminal conviction. The universities or colleges may then ask you for more details.

NB: Applicants or their advisers who wish to declare additional material information but do not wish to do so in the UCAS application should write direct to admissions officers at the universities and colleges listed on the application or at any other institution considering their application.

Disability/special needs

Universities and colleges welcome students with disabilities and will try to meet their needs wherever they reasonably can. The information you give in the application will help them do this. UCAS will also use it to monitor progress in equal opportunities in higher education.

If you have a disability, special needs (including dyslexia or another specific learning difficulty) or a medical condition, you should select the most appropriate option from the list below.

- No disability (if you do not have a disability, special needs or a medical condition, select 'No disability').
- You have a social/communication impairment such as Asperger's syndrome/other autistic spectrum disorder.
- You are blind or have a serious visual impairment uncorrected by glasses.
- You are deaf or have a serious hearing impairment.
- You have a long-standing illness or health condition such as cancer, HIV, diabetes, chronic heart disease or epilepsy.
- You have a mental health condition such as depression, schizophrenia or anxiety disorder.
- You have a specific learning difficulty such as dyslexia, dyspraxia or ADHD.
- You have a physical impairment or mobility issues, such as difficulty using your arms, or use a wheelchair or crutches.
- You have a disability, impairment or medical condition that is not listed above.
- You have two or more impairments and/or disabling medical conditions.

Further information on these options is given on Apply.

A space is included for you to provide details of any disabilities, special needs or medical conditions that affect you. Some applicants are reluctant to fill this in – either because they do not want to draw attention to themselves or because they think their chances of acceptance may be adversely affected. This is not the case. Universities and colleges need to know about any measures they may need to take to cope effectively with your needs, and if you supply this information it will help them make suitable preparations so that they can:

- make necessary allowances (for example, they may be willing to lower entry requirements to allow for serious difficulties; they may need to provide you with readers or interpreters, or give you extra time to complete your course)
- ensure that any additional facilities or equipment are available (adapted accommodation, for example).

It is in your interest to give all relevant information in this section. It will not affect the university's or college's decision regarding your suitability for the course.

If you claim special consideration on account of dyslexia, be prepared to provide independent evidence (usually a psychologist's report). Allowances will be made but admissions tutors will need to be convinced that you can keep up with the work required.

Other information

TOEFL number or IELTS number

If you have registered for or already hold either of these English language tests (for international students), enter your number in the relevant field.

Passport details

If you need a visa to enter the UK to study, you are asked to provide the number, place of issue, issue date and expiry date of your passport. If you do not yet have a passport, you will be asked to send on this information once you have obtained one.

Finally, tick 'Section completed' and click 'Save' to save all the information entered in 'Personal details' before moving on to the next section.

13| Additional information

This section of the application only appears if you answered 'Yes' to your permanent home being in the UK. It covers:

- activities in preparation for higher education
- whether you have been in care
- parental education
- whether you would like to receive correspondence in Welsh
- ethnic origin
- national identity
- occupational background.

Do not worry about the last three (ethnic origin, national identity and occupational background). This information about you is designed to help UCAS and the universities and colleges monitor applications and equal opportunities, not to inform them during the selection process. They do not have these details until after they have considered your application.

Activities in preparation for higher education

Summer schools and similar courses are held throughout the year and are also known as Saturday university, campus days, summer academies, taster courses and booster courses.

If you have taken part in one or more of these activities (or anything similar), select the relevant option from the list and give more details of what you did in your personal statement.

You can enter a maximum of two activities here; if you have attended more than two, list the two most recently attended, together with the appropriate start date(s). Details of any activities not entered in this section should be explained in your personal statement.

Some relevant activities are listed below.

- ASPIRENorth – promoting greater participation in the north of Scotland: www.aspirenorth.co.uk.
- Aberystwyth Summer University: www.aber.ac.uk/en/widening-participation/schoolscolleges/summer-uni.
- Academic Enrichment programme – University of Birmingham: www.birmingham.ac.uk/teachers/pupil-opportunities/post-16/year-12-academic-enrichment-programme.aspx.

- Aim Higher London South: http://aimhigherlondonsouth.org.uk.
- Aim Higher West Midlands: www.aimhigherwm.ac.uk.
- Discovering Queen's programme – a widening participation project in Northern Ireland: www.qub.ac.uk/alpine/ ALPINE/5_2_2_e1.htm.
- FOCUS West: www.focuswest.org.uk.
- Future Quest: www.futurequest.org.uk.
- Higher Education Insight (HEI) programme: www.birmingham.ac.uk/teachers/pupil-opportunities/outside-west-midlands/Year-12-higher-education-insight.aspx.
- Lothians Equal Access Programme for Schools (LEAPS): www.leapsonline.org.
- LIFT OFF (Tayside): www.lift-off.org.uk.
- Nottingham Potential Summer School: www.nottingham.ac.uk/schoolsliaison/services/nottingham-potential-summer-school.aspx.
- NU Entry – Northumbria University: www.northumbria.ac.uk/study-at-northumbria/information-for-schools-and-colleges/northumbria-university-supported-entry-scheme.
- Pathway Opportunity Programme – Queen's University Belfast: www.qub.ac.uk/directorates/sgc/wpu/PathwayOpportunity Programme.
- Reaching Wider initiative in Wales: www.reachingwider.ac.uk.
- Realising Opportunities: www.realisingopportunities.ac.uk.
- Routes to the Profession (r2p): www.birmingham.ac.uk/teachers/pupil-opportunities/post-16/routes-to-professions.aspx.
- Seren Network: http://gov.wales/topics/educationandskills/learningproviders/seren/?lang=en.
- Sutton Trust: www.suttontrust.com.
- UniTracks – The Warwick Young Achievers' Programme: https://warwick.ac.uk/study/outreach/whatweoffer/unitracks.
- University of Oxford's UNIQ summer schools: www.uniq.ox.ac.uk.
- Villiers Park post-16 residential courses: www.villierspark.org.uk.
- Vinspired: https://vinspired.com.
- Warwick in London – pre-university taster courses: https://warwick.ac.uk/insite/news/intnews2/warwick_in_london_pre_uni_taster_sessions.
- Other. This category includes widening access programmes and summer schools run by many universities in the UK. More information is available from your local university.

You will also need to say when and where you went to the summer school or other programme. You can say what you learned from your visit in your personal statement.

Care

Universities and colleges may be able to offer extra resources or support, for example with out-of-term accommodation, for those who have been in care at some stage. If you choose 'Yes' in response to this field, you will be asked to say how long you were in care.

Parental education

You will be asked to indicate whether or not either of your parents, or your step-parents or guardians, have any higher education qualifications, such as degrees, diplomas or certificates of higher education. If you are unsure, select 'Don't know' from the drop-down list. If you do not wish to disclose this information, you can select 'I prefer not to say'.

Ethnic origin

You are asked to state your ethnic origin, or the category that broadly corresponds with the origin of your recent forebears. Carefully read the options in the drop-down list, and then select one. The options are:

- white
- gypsy, traveller or Irish traveller
- black – Caribbean
- black – African
- black – other background
- Asian – Indian
- Asian – Pakistani
- Asian – Bangladeshi
- Asian – Chinese
- Asian – other background
- mixed – white and black Caribbean
- mixed – white and black African
- mixed – white and Asian
- mixed – other background
- Arab
- other ethnic background
- I prefer not to say.

You must enter one of the options listed, even if it is 'I prefer not to say', or you will not be able to register your application as finished.

National identity

You will be asked to classify your national identity. This is different from ethnicity and nationality and can be based on many things, including, for example, culture, language or ancestry/family history.

You will need to describe your national identity using the options listed below. You can use either one option, for example 'Welsh', or two options if you feel you have dual national identity, for example 'English' and 'Scottish', or 'Irish' and 'Other' if you are Irish with a national identity not listed. If you feel that you have more than two national identities, you should select 'Other' for one or both options.

- British
- English
- Irish
- Scottish
- Welsh
- Other
- I prefer not to say.

Correspondence in Welsh

If you have applied to one or more universities or colleges in Wales and you want them to correspond with you in Welsh, select 'Yes'. Note that you need to do this even if your whole application is in Welsh.

If you write your application in Welsh you will automatically receive correspondence in Welsh from UCAS. Since this section is viewed only by UK residents, other applicants unfortunately do not have the opportunity to use Apply to request correspondence in Welsh. If you are in this position, you need to make requests directly to the relevant institutions.

Finally, tick 'Section completed' and click 'Save' to save all the information entered in 'Additional information' before moving on to the next section.

Occupational background

If you are aged under 21, you should give the occupation of your parent, step-parent or guardian who earns the most. If she or he is retired, give their most recent occupation. If you are 21 or over, you should give your own occupation. Enter at least three characters of the job title in the search box and select the job title you want. If you prefer not to give this information, please enter: 'I prefer not to say'.

This information is converted into occupational classifications based on those used by the Office for National Statistics, and will be used to help monitor participation in higher education across all parts of society. Please note that this information will not be released to your chosen universities or colleges until after a decision has been made regarding your application.

14| Choices

This is one of the most important parts of your application, and it represents the culmination of your research into higher education. It is often best to leave entering details of the courses you are applying to until you have completed all the factual information required and worked out your personal statement.

Specifically, this section covers the following fields of the Choices screen (see Figure 4 opposite):

- Institution code
- Course code
- Campus code
- Start date
- Further details
- Live at home while studying?
- Point of entry.

You are allowed a maximum of five course applications, which should be obvious in light of the space provided. You can apply to fewer than five if you wish, and can add other courses until the end of June as long as you haven't already accepted any offers. If you applied to only one course initially you will be allowed to add up to four additional choices, but only if you pay the difference between the single and multiple application fees (£18 and £24 respectively – see Chapter 18 for more information on payments).

Institution code

To make it absolutely clear which courses you are applying to, you need to include details both of the courses and of the universities or colleges that run them. Apply gives you the option of entering these details using course and institution names or codes. You can either find the relevant code using the UCAS search tool on www.ucas.com or find the relevant institution name using Apply. If you opt for the latter method, click on 'See list'; this will bring up an alphabetical list from which you can select the relevant code(s) by the name of the institution(s) to which you wish to apply.

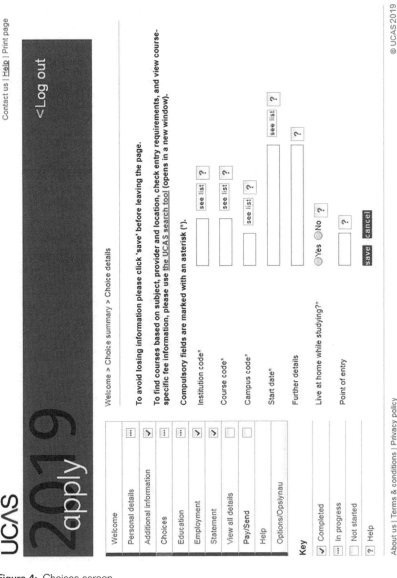

Figure 4: Choices screen

Course code

As before, you can find out the code for the course you wish to apply to via the UCAS website or by clicking 'See list' next to the relevant space in Apply and selecting your course from the alphabetical list that appears (only courses offered at your chosen institution will be displayed for you to select from).

Apply will bring up an error message if you enter a course code that is not recognised, but it is still possible to apply to a course unintentionally if you do not double-check that the code you enter corresponds to the actual course that interests you. Make sure you have access to course information (such as that on the UCAS website) and click 'Save' after each entry. This helps you check for any mistakes.

If you select a course that requires applicants to attend an interview or audition or to provide a portfolio or evidence of work, a message will be displayed on screen to inform you of this.

Campus code

Some courses are taught at franchised institutions, i.e. away from the main university or college. If this is the case for one of your chosen courses, you will need to enter a campus code (for example, Argyll College of the University of Highlands and Islands is represented by the letter A), as in Figure 5 opposite. Enter the relevant code by clicking on 'See list' next to the campus code column. If you are not sure whether a campus code is needed, you can click on 'Save' and see whether Apply highlights the campus box to be filled in. Even if your course is available at only one campus, you may need to select the 'Main' site from the list.

> **TIP!**
>
> Don't forget that you can make insurance subject choices as alternatives to your applications to medicine, dentistry or veterinary medicine or science (see Chapter 8).

Start date

A list of available start dates will be displayed when you click on 'See list'. If you want to apply at this stage for deferred entry (that is, starting your course in 2020 rather than 2019), you should select the correct date from the list. More information on deferred entry is given in Chapter 8. Your personal statement (see Chapter 17) gives you the chance to explain why you want to defer entry.

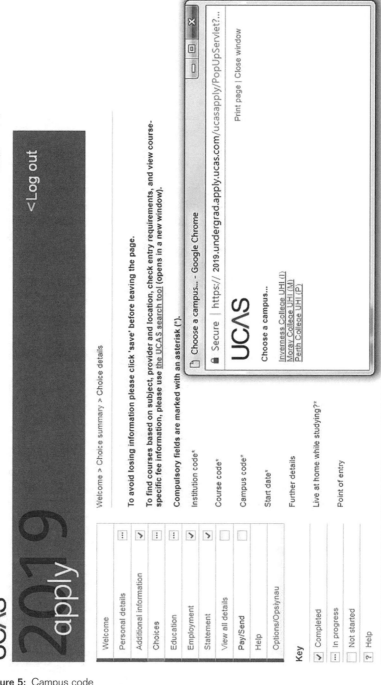

Contact us | Help | Print page

<Log out

UCAS
2019
apply

Welcome > Choice summary > Choice details

To avoid losing information please click 'save' before leaving the page.

To find courses based on subject, provider and location, check entry requirements, and view course-specific fee information, please use the UCAS search tool (opens in a new window).

Compulsory fields are marked with an asterisk (*).

Welcome		
Personal details	::	✓
Additional information	::	
Choices	::	
Education	::	✓
Employment		✓
Statement		✓
View all details		☐
Pay/Send		☐
Help		
Options/Opsiynau		

Institution code*

Course code*

Campus code*

Start date*

Further details

Live at home while studying?*

Point of entry

Key
✓ Completed
:: In progress
☐ Not started
? Help

About us | Terms & conditions | Privacy policy

Choose a campus... – Google Chrome

⊟ ⊡ ✕

🔒 Secure | https:// 2019.undergrad.apply.ucas.com/ucasapply/PopUpServlet?...

Print page | Close window

UCAS

Choose a campus...

Inverness College UHI (I)
Moray College UHI (M)
Perth College UHI (P)

© UCAS 2019

Figure 5: Campus code

> **TIP!**
>
> It is no use applying for 2020 entry in 2018/19 if some of your exams won't be taken until 2020. Even though your start date is deferred, a final decision on this application has to be taken by August 2019, unless otherwise agreed by the university or college. Furthermore, you are not allowed to keep a deferred place at a university or college and then apply the following year to other institutions of the same kind. UCAS will intercept and cancel such applications!

Further details

On many UCAS applications this part is left blank. But further information may be requested by institutions and should be provided. Check the UCAS search tool on www.ucas.com or the university or college prospectus to find out whether this is the case. The sort of information you may need to give could include:

- duration of the course (three- or four-year course)
- minor, subsidiary or first-year course option choice
- specialisations within your chosen course
- Qualified Teacher Status
- previous applications
- if you are applying to Oxford and have selected a permanent private hall (rather than a college with a campus code), this section can be used to state which hall you have chosen.

Living at home while studying?

Choose 'Yes' if you are planning to live at home while attending a particular university or college, or 'No' if you will need accommodation information from the university or college.

Point of entry

If you plan to join the course at the beginning of the first year, leave this part blank. If you think you may qualify for credit transfer or entry with advanced standing (entry at second-year level or perhaps third-year level in Scotland), you should check this possibility with the institutions to which you wish to apply before completing your application. You may then indicate this to the universities and colleges by entering '2' or '3' (i.e. the year of proposed entry) in the relevant box for each application to which this applies.

15| Education

It is essential that you include information about your education to date in your application. This helps to give institutions a better idea of who you are, as well as providing them with evidence of your academic attainment and potential. They will, of course, also use the information you give here to put together conditional offers.

Specifically, this section covers:

- schools and colleges attended
- qualifications (both those already attained and those yet to be taken).

Schools and colleges attended

Apply will ask you to add details of the schools and colleges (including any schools and colleges overseas) that you have attended – see Figure 6 on page 142. You must enter at least one school or college. Click on 'Add new school/college centre' and use the 'Find' button to search for your institution; the exam centre number will be entered automatically. Higher education and overseas institutions do not usually have exam centre numbers, so if you have studied at one you will need to leave the exam centre number box blank. A warning will appear asking you to enter a number, but you can still move on to the next screen to continue your application.

Enter all the secondary schools, colleges and universities you have attended, up to a maximum of 10. If you have attended more than 10, enter the 10 most recent. If you have spent any time at a higher education institution you must say so, and be prepared for questions about it should you be called for interview.

If you cannot find your school, click on 'My school/centre is not listed here'. You can then type the name of the school into the box.

Select the dates you attended from the drop-down lists. You will also need to enter the exam centre number. You can obtain this from your school or by looking at your examination certificates. If you have been home-schooled for all of your secondary education, click on 'Find' and enter a term such as 'Home'. If a suitable option is not there, click on 'My school/centre is not listed here' and then type 'Home-schooled' into the box.

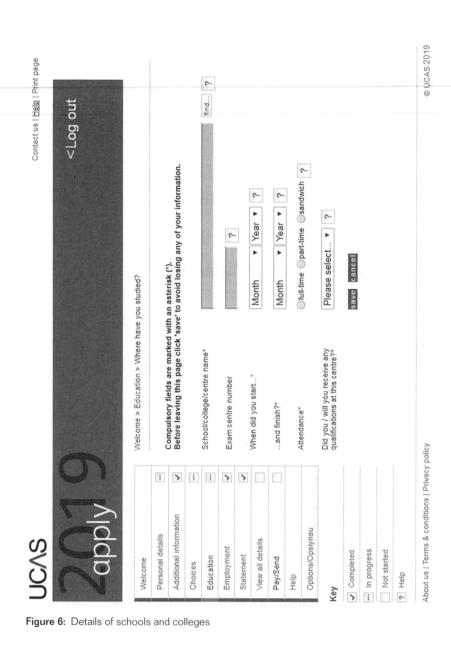

Figure 6: Details of schools and colleges

Qualifications

As outlined in Chapter 6, this part of the application is crucial, as it is bound to be scrutinised carefully by admissions tutors. There are so many different kinds of qualification that you may already have, or may be planning to take, that it is also a potentially confusing area – you need to make sure that you include all the relevant information as outlined below.

Entering your qualifications

After entering the details of the schools and colleges you have attended, you will be presented with a list of them and a link beneath each one to 'Add qualifications'.

Check that everything (dates of attendance, etc.) is correct and click on 'Add qualifications' to enter the qualifications that you took at that school or college. The link will take you through to a list of qualifications that your school or college teaches, for example:

* A level
* Advanced VCE
* BTEC Diploma
* Irish Leaving Certificate
* GCSE
* European Baccalaureate.

If your qualification is not listed, enter its name into the search box. A list of qualifications with that name will appear underneath. Click on a qualification that you have taken (or will be taking – see below). This will take you to a screen where you can enter all the details of the qualification.

> **TIP!**
>
> You can enter the country where you took a qualification in the search box to list all the qualifications for that country.

For example, for a GCSE you will need to enter the subject, date of certification, awarding body and grade. If you have not yet completed a qualification, leave the grade box as 'Pending'. You will also be asked to enter information about the units you have taken and unit grades you have achieved in qualifications that have been completed and certificated, such as GCE AS exams. However, entering unit details for GCE AS or A levels is optional.

Once you have completed this screen you then have the option to add another subject for that particular qualification by clicking 'Save and add similar'. When you have no more subjects to add, click 'Save'. At this point, if anything is amiss, you will be told by the green text. If everything is in order, you will be shown the qualifications and subjects you have already entered and given the option to 'Add qualifications'. If you have anything to add, click on this and start the process again.

Once you have entered all the qualifications you have completed or are yet to complete, tick 'Section completed' and click 'Save'.

If you entered a Scottish qualification, you will be prompted to enter your Scottish Candidate Number. If you do not know your number, ask your college or check your exam certificate.

Some BTEC qualifications will also ask for your BTEC Registration Number; check with your school or college if you're not sure what this is.

Putting the right information on your UCAS application is important. Incorrect or incomplete information can cause problems for your university or college and could result in an inaccurate or delayed decision.

You can return to the education area of your application, to edit or add to the entries already made, up to the point when you submit your application through your UCAS coordinator.

Which qualifications to include?

Qualifications you have already received

You should list all qualifications for which you have received certification from the awarding body (this will usually include GCSEs, Scottish Nationals 4 and 5, Intermediate GNVQs and so on). Include all the qualifications you have taken, even if you didn't pass them. You must not conceal anything because you will have to declare at a later stage that you have entered complete and accurate information. You may be asked to supply original certificates to support the qualifications listed in your application at any time during the application process. You must include details of these qualifications even if you are planning to retake, whether completely or only in part. (You can explain your reasons for retaking in your personal statement.)

If you are a mature student with no formal qualifications, enter 'No formal qualifications'. (See page 158 for advice on how you can address this issue in your personal statement.) If you are hoping to enter university or college via APL or APEL, you should contact your chosen institution before applying to UCAS.

> **TIP!**
>
> Mature students should complete this section as fully as possible – many forget to list their present college.

If you are an international student, you need to give full details of all your qualifications in the original language. Do not try to provide a UK equivalent. If your first language is not English but your qualifications were completely or partly assessed in English, make this clear. You should also provide details of any English language tests you have taken or plan to take, giving dates, titles and any syllabus codes. Send a copy of all transcripts, certificates or other proof of your qualifications direct to each university or college you apply to, quoting the title and code number of the course and your UCAS Personal ID once you have submitted your application to UCAS. Do not, however, send anything of this sort to UCAS.

> **TIP!**
>
> If you feel that there are genuine reasons why some of your grades were lower than expected, make sure that the person who is going to write your reference is aware of this and can explain the reason.

Qualifications you are studying for

You must also enter details of all qualifications that you are studying for now and those for which you are awaiting results. These may include A levels, Scottish Highers and Advanced Highers, BTEC qualifications, NVQs, Access courses and so on.

> **TIP!**
>
> If you have one, you should take your full Progress File (a record of your personal development, skills development and achievements) with you if invited for interview. If you wish, send a brief summary (not the full record) direct to the institution, quoting your Personal ID. You should be prepared to discuss and explain what your Progress File comprises, and how it was developed.

> **TIP!**
>
> Help and advice on completing the Education section are available at www.ucas.com/ucas/undergraduate/apply-and-track/filling-your-ucas-undergraduate-application.

16 | Employment

It is very useful for admissions tutors to know if you have had a job. This can be particularly helpful if you have worked in an area relevant to your application or chosen career. Paid full-time and part-time jobs (including weekend jobs) should be included, but only if they have been continued for a reasonable period. Even if the jobs you held were just to earn pocket money, an admissions tutor will see this as a broadening of your experience. Note that institutions undertake not to contact previous employers for a reference without your permission.

If you have information to enter, click on 'Add an employer' in the employment area of Apply. Then fill in the employer's name (i.e. the company name) and address, your job description, start and end dates, and whether it is/was full or part time. If the job you are entering is where you are employed currently, you do not need to enter a date under 'When did you finish?' Click 'Save' to take you to the employment summary screen and then – when you are ready – tick 'Section completed' and click 'Save'.

If you do not have anything to enter in this section, you just need to tick 'Section completed' and click 'Save'.

17| Personal statement

This section is crucial because it is the only part of the application where you have the chance to select and emphasise points about yourself and to explain to admissions tutors why you are interested in your chosen subject(s). This is your chance to impress and convince admissions tutors to offer you a place. Personal statements have a maximum length of 4,000 characters (47 lines) and a minimum of 1,000 characters – so you need to think very carefully about exactly what you want to say in the limited space provided. You can click on 'Save' at any time to update the line and character count.

What are admissions tutors looking for?

Factual information

The admissions tutors will want to know about:

- your career aspirations
- your reasons for choosing the course(s)
- relevant background or experience, which may include work experience/work shadowing, practical activity in music or theatre, attendance on courses, time abroad, etc. (evidence of practical experience may be vital to the success of an application to a medical or veterinary school, and may also significantly help your application if you are applying for some management and engineering courses)
- any interests you may have (e.g. Duke of Edinburgh's Award, charity fundraising, painting, potholing, positions of responsibility) – these may not seem strictly relevant to the course, but they help to give an impression of you as a person
- the name of any sponsor you may have. Relatively few students are sponsored through their course and you will not be at a disadvantage if you have nothing to include in this respect. Universities and colleges are keen to know, however, if you have been able to secure this form of financial support. If you have applied for sponsorship but do not yet know whether you have been successful, say where you have applied.

Reading between the lines

Your statement will convey more about you than just the bare facts. The way you present the facts will give valuable clues about other qualities such as critical thinking and communication skills.

Analytical skills

Admissions tutors are usually looking for students who can analyse their current experience. A common weakness is that applicants tend to describe what they are doing now rather than analysing their current experiences, relating them to what they hope to get from higher education and their future career prospects.

Alongside the descriptive approach tends to be a listing of data already entered in the application (e.g. present studies) or details of apparently unrelated hobbies. Hobbies are an important part of your statement, but they need to be analysed in the context of how they have contributed to your skills or personal development in a way that would be an indicator of success on the courses to which you have applied.

Communication skills

The text and presentation of your statement provide the admissions tutor with an indication of your communication skills – both basic grammar and spelling and your ability to express information and ideas clearly.

Maturity

A good statement provides evidence of maturity of thought and a sense of responsibility. If you intend to study away from home, it is important to show that you have these attributes, as they indicate that you will be likely to adapt well to your new environment.

> **TIP!**
>
> It is difficult for an applicant who has selected a wide range of disparate courses to give feasible reasons for having done so, which is why this approach is not recommended.

Top tips

Impression. Think about the impression you want to give – you need to make yourself sound interesting, bright, mature and eager to learn.

Structure. Organise what you want to say into a logical structure and make sure that everything you say is clear and concise. Use subheadings if you think it will help.

Length. Do not try to pack too much in – it can get confusing. Hit the reader with your main point, and do not worry about filling up all 47 lines – rambling on simply to use all the space is likely to be counterproductive.

Relevance. Explain why each point you mention is relevant. Do not unnecessarily repeat material that already appears on the application form.

Honesty. It is imperative that you are honest and specific. If necessary, be selective – there are only 24 hours in a day, and claiming too much is not always a good idea.

Accuracy. Check your spelling. Apply does not have a spell-check facility, so it is recommended that you word-process your statement as a Word document and spell-check it first, then copy and paste it into the relevant Apply area. Get someone else to read it through, too – it's sometimes hard to spot your own mistakes, and computer spell-checkers are not infallible.

Placing 'leads'. Admissions tutors are likely to use your statement as a source of questions if they call you for interview. You should therefore only mention things you are prepared to talk about at an interview. If there is something you would particularly like to be asked to discuss, you can give the interviewer a lead by mentioning it in your statement.

And finally ...

Check up on yourself. Read critically through everything you have written. Try to imagine you are the admissions tutor, trying to pick holes in what you've said. You may also find it useful to work with friends and read through each other's drafts – you will be surprised how often a friend will say to you, 'But haven't you forgotten ...?'

> **TIP!**
>
> You can find advice on completing your personal statement at: www.ucas.com/personalstatement and in the book, *How to Create a Winning Personal Statement*, Trotman Education.

> ### Advice on completing the personal statement
>
> 'It can be very difficult when ideas begin to flow to limit yourself to the permitted number of characters. So, the statement needs to be carefully and tightly worded in order to include everything you want the person reading it to know about you. This is your opportunity to impress the university or college. You are selling yourself to that person and telling them why you are the best person for that course and why they should offer you a place.
>
> 'I advise putting points in the following order:

- What your chosen subject is and why you are interested in it.
- Anything you have done that is not curriculum based to show your understanding and to prove you are passionate about it – for example events or optional lectures you have been to, journals, websites or blogs that you follow.
- Work experience.
- Examples of other interests and responsibilities. You can use things like part-time work, voluntary work, school or college responsibilities.

'Under the last two headings don't simply write a list. Explain what you learned from them – anything that is relevant to the course you are applying for and anything that has helped you to develop as a person.

'Finally, you should write one or two sentences as a summary, reminding the reader why you should be given a place.'

Alison Wilson, Schools and Colleges Liaison Coordinator,
University of Winchester

TIP!

Save your work regularly to keep the line count updated, and click to preview your statement. Click 'Edit' to make changes, and tick 'Section completed' then click 'Save' to complete.

Creating a winning personal statement

Amazingly, every year there are a few applicants who leave the statement section completely blank. Obviously this is inadvisable, to say the least! But many others do themselves no good simply as a result of the way they present information.

Sample good personal statements

Alice, International Marketing (3,879 characters, with spaces)

Marketing interests me because it is something that is constantly changing. For example, in the past, primarily newspapers were used for advertising and marketing, but this is not the case for the future. It is important to observe trends and help the brand to evolve to meet the changing market. I have a particular interest in digital marketing as I believe that is the future.

I see marketing as a rapidly evolving global business environment. Marketing has been something I have become very interested in during the last few years. My interest was strengthened by studying Business Studies at GCSE. It was then that I realised that my future career should be in marketing. Having taken part in work experience at Stannah Stairlifts, I gained a valuable insight into how an international business is successfully run within a positive working environment. An example of this is that while I was at Stannah, they received a complaint from a customer, and they taught me how to respond and resolve the problem to the customer's satisfaction, and the customer is likely to return.

My A level subjects have helped me to grow as a person and will help me capitalise on the fast moving and ever-changing demands that marketing places upon the individual, the team, the suppliers and ultimately the consumer. Psychology shows me people from a different angle and how to view the world around me from different perspectives. I have also learnt how to analyse and interpret data, which I know is essential in advertising and marketing. Chemistry is enlightening, and I show clear perseverance and that I am able to study independently, as well as with my peers while taking part in practical work. In addition to meeting deadlines, I am finding my individual investigation interesting and am coping well with its demands. It is teaching me about managing my time and providing me with the knowledge of many skills that will help me in later life. Taking mathematics allows me to learn skills such as data collation and analytical skills. This was strengthened with an AS Statistics module which has taught me how to further enhance my analytical skills.

While at Taunton School I took part in Newton's Den which was our school's version of Dragons Den. We worked in groups to a brief of creating something to benefit the school. This developed my presentation skills when having to present to a panel of judges as well as working in a group.

Through taking part in hockey and netball matches on Saturday afternoons as well as swimming galas, I know the value of team work and the hard work and dedication it takes to make these things happen. This I believe will help me to be successful at university. I also had to be flexible to play at short notice and have the confidence to do so when asked. I took a leading role on many occasions, such as organising the swimming team for my school house. All these soft skills are important for one to be successful in business.

Through travelling to places such as Dubai, Canada, South Africa and Europe, I have gained access to different cultures and can appreciate that marketing strategies need to adapt to different cultures. When I see advertisements on television I think about how I would do it differently or sometimes I will see a product advertised and wonder how I would target it to students my age. My studies at university will harness my skills and knowledge gained so far as I am a self-motivated individual. At university I will strengthen existing skills, such as Meta skills, and learn a range of new ones. These will enable me to work even more effectively in the workplace and in my career in advertising and marketing.

I believe that marketing is a career path that has endless opportunities and provides life skills as well as being full of exciting prospects.

Holly, Anthropology and Innovation (3,992 characters, with spaces)

When I was 16, I raised £4,000 for materials and travelled to rural Romania to build a house for a homeless family. The people that I encountered there had virtually nothing. It was then that my fascination with human kind, and thus anthropology, forced me to first question why.

Why is it that the poverty rate in Romania is 38% while in the UK it is only 16%? How is it that a country with outstanding natural resources has such prevailing destitution in comparison to its European neighbours? Toylan Rotaru theorises in his paper 'Poverty in Transition and Transition in Poverty' that Romania is a victim of communism crippled by a corrupt government. I do not dismiss this argument as inaccurate; however, I think that the governmental corruption is just a symptom of the problem and that Rotaru's argument does not adequately address the fundamental aetiology. Jared Diamond examines the primal causes of global wealth inequality in his book *Guns, Germs and Steel*, such as food production, the domestication of animals, pathogenic immunity and the harnessing of steel. I believe that an amalgamation of these two arguments is necessary to draw a logical conclusion. The exploration of issues such as this has always appealed to me and led me to undertake an Extended Project titled: 'To What Extent does Smiling Contribute to our General Wellbeing'. In this project I explored the impacts that smiling has on our mental health, careers and relationships. I also examined the significance of smiling in different cultures and discovered the disparate connotations that it has globally. I am exploring anthropological texts to cement my ideas on key issues to allow me to further develop my knowledge of the subject.

I believe that learning the language is the only way to truly understand a culture. My study of French A level has allowed me to experience this cultural immersion while inspiring me to research the ethnography of communication, particularly the works of Dell Hymes. In 2014 I completed a work placement in France; this highlighted the subtle cultural differences between the UK and France, even concerning these proximate countries. I plan to learn further languages in the future, initially Mandarin. Biology and Chemistry have allowed me to maintain a breadth of knowledge and understanding of scientific principles. An area of biology that I am particularly moved by is the study of HIV AIDS. This resulted in me applying and succeeding in being selected to travel to Lesotho for 12 weeks as an ambassador for the 'Coaching to Hope' programme, which aims to raise awareness and collect data about HIV AIDS prevention through sport. In addition to helping the communities I will encounter, this opportunity will enable me to deepen my understanding of people culturally through ethnographic research and natural observation.

I have played hockey and netball at first team school and county level and have also completed the Gold Duke of Edinburgh award. Experiencing how individuals behave under pressure and the factors that contribute to a team's dynamic fascinates me. Having read a variety of anthropological texts it is evident that a consensus is seldom reached between individuals in the field. My experiences as a team member and as the chair of the debating society have equipped me with the ability to form my own objective opinions and question those of others. I have also learned perseverance and dedication through music.

Being Head Girl at my school allowed me to develop many skills, such as public speaking, personal communication and time management. During my gap year I am gaining skills that I am certain will prove invaluable to me as an anthropology undergraduate. In addition to travelling to Lesotho, I intend to work in many different environments to add to my appreciation of socially and culturally diverse communities.

I truly believe than an anthropology degree will inspire me and allow me to further my exploration of cultural diversity.

Holly, Biology (3,968 characters, with spaces)

The human body and mind are constantly evolving due to cell mutations and adaptations to changes in the environment; this complex nature of the human anatomy and nervous system has enticed me into wanting to study this course. The fact that I will be constantly revealing new information and always furthering my knowledge I find particularly exciting.

The anatomy and cell biology aspect of my A level course and work experience has engaged me the most as there are many questions left unanswered, such as in-depth detail on how the muscular and nervous system interlink to provide our movement. This has led me to investigate these areas further to ensure I have a full understanding of them. Furthermore, learning about cells, biological molecules and different organ functions at A level has fascinated me, as they all interrelate and can be applied to learning why different mammalians act in a variety of ways and how they adapt to different diseases and environmental conditions. Through my university course I hope to achieve an understanding of different anatomies and cellular functions, as well as furthering my interest in molecular biology and biochemistry.

Cells and the nervous system have captivated me most during my A level Biology study, as I can relate the knowledge to how my body functions. Cells and nerves are so complex and intricate that I am intrigued as to why certain bodily functions take place in terms of chemistry. Taking A level Chemistry gave me my first introduction to biochemistry, looking at amines and carboxylic acid groups in relation to proteins. Chemistry gave me a more logical approach when looking at biological molecules and the reactions within the body. *High Price* is a book relating to neuroscience that helped me to link the chemistry of the body with how the nervous system works and the physiological effects nerves have on a person. When undertaking work experience at the Royal Marsden Hospital I was able to investigate more biochemistry in the pharmaceutical department and furthered my interest in the anatomy and complexity of the human body. I was also fortunate to gain experience with two different types of physiotherapists; Gill Mayberry works with horses and John Harris who is a human chiropractor/physiotherapist. Furthermore, I also undertook work experience at St Helier emergency department, shadowing a nurse who worked in Accident & Emergency. Through their work I was able to see the differences in the anatomy of humans and animals; and, conversely, how evolution has led to biological changes that can cause a variety of disease and ailments. These experiences enabled me to gain more knowledge in anatomy and biochemistry and furthered my drive to succeed in this course.

Achieving my Gold Duke of Edinburgh has given me communication and exploration skills which will help when undertaking research tasks. The nature of the challenge has now made me more determined to succeed in future ultimatums. Furthermore, I was a mentor to younger peers, as well as coaching a younger team in netball and being a prefect. All these roles gave me a large amount of responsibility and improved my interpersonal skills, which I can take forward onto my course. I have been in the first team for hockey, netball, swimming and rugby since the beginning of my senior school career, which has given me the understanding of the necessity for teamwork and logical thinking. These sports have given me the chance to develop my skills and enhanced my drive to succeed; this will help me to think logically during the course.

I believe I possess the logical skills and drive that would allow me to thrive on a physiology course. I am independent and hard-working and have a lot of initiative that will be needed to complete the degree competently. The work experience I have gained, as well as my volunteering at the RSPCA and further reading of the *Biological Science Review*, has given me even more motivation to succeed on a biology related degree of this nature.

Chris, Industrial Economics (3,983 characters, with spaces)

I decided to study economics in order to understand the economic system in which companies and nations operate and contribute to their effective functioning.

I made this decision due to my interest in applied mathematics, global and economic current affairs, my travelling experience in developing countries and my internships in the nuclear and oil sectors. From a degree in economics I hope to gain a thorough understanding of economic principles to prepare me for a career where my skills will be of benefit to society.

I find the application of mathematics to social science fascinating. A level Mathematics gives me an excellent basis for the quantitative methods in economics. I have proven my aptitude for problem solving by gaining a Silver Award in the Senior Maths Challenge. By studying A level Physics, I have learned to think laterally due to the synoptic nature of the course. I have decided to use my gap year to both improve on my existing A level grades as well as study A level Italian. This will add a further plus-point to my CV as I would be able to use Italian in a future job. I regularly read economic and business news in the Italian press and follow Italy's developments with interest.

Family holidays have taken me to emerging countries where I observed many problems, such as the mismanagement of South Africa's natural resources, and the difficulties of water extraction and distribution in Kenya, which could be solved by applying economics and business skills. A recent trip across India made me realise how social and political divides can hamper the economic and social development of a subcontinent with a lot of potential. It opened my eyes to the fact that, using my prospective macro- and micro-economics skills as well as my determination and enthusiasm, I could make a real difference to people's lives in future.

During the summer of 2016 I worked for the Culham Centre for Fusion Energy in Oxford, where I analysed data for Dr Fulvio Militello. Here I was taught the basic ideas behind nuclear fusion and learned how economics could be applied to make difficult decisions in the energy field. For instance, I believe that Europe and North America would be better advised to invest in bringing the seminal fusion technology to the commercial stage, rather than subsidising technologies such as the current fission reactors. Furthermore, I think that the UK should be focusing on harnessing its tidal energy to supply the country with clean and financially viable power.

In the summer of 2017 I worked for AGR Tracks, a global oil service company where I learned how the economic aspects of oil prospection, extraction and refining are vital to making key investment decisions regarding long term and capital investment projects. It was interesting to find out about the advantages and disadvantages of foreign investment in developing countries.

In terms of my extracurricular activities, I started playing hockey when I came to England in 2012 and, as well as representing Millfield College, I trained for the Somerset hockey team until 2016. Later I was a member of the first XI hockey team at St George's College. Playing required stamina and commitment; it also developed my teamwork greatly.

I have completed the Duke of Edinburgh Gold Award, including the expedition phase, which involved orienteering, trip planning and mental endurance and for the volunteering phase I have been coaching hockey to 13–15-year-olds. This experience has helped improve my communication skills and my ability to manage people and time.

From January to April 2018, I shall be in Canada on a ski patrol course. This course will require me to pass the tests to qualify as a ski patroller, further developing my decision-making skills, communication and making wise use of the responsibility and trust given to me.

I look forward to studying economics at university and am striving towards getting the grades needed to study at a respectable institution.

TIP!

If you want to supply more information than the statement space allows, once your application has been processed and you have received your welcome email you can send information directly to your chosen universities or colleges, quoting your Personal ID. (Do not send it to UCAS.)

Specific advice

The personal statement is especially important in subjects such as creative and performing arts. Say what you have done, seen or heard – do not be one of the music applicants who do not actually mention their chosen instrument!

Applicants for teacher training, medicine, veterinary science, dentistry or physiotherapy courses should be sure to give details of work experience (including locations and dates).

If you are currently studying for a vocational or occupational qualification with which admissions tutors may be relatively unfamiliar, explain the relevance of your studies to the course(s) for which you are applying.

If you are an international student, explain why you want to study in the UK. Can you provide evidence that you will be able to complete a course run and taught in English?

If you are a sporting person, give details of your achievements. 'I play tennis' adds little; 'I play tennis for the county' shows that you are committed to something you excel in.

If you plan to take a gap year, it is advisable to cover your reasons for doing so in your statement. Remember that anything you say is likely to be used as a basis for questions at interview. The two examples below show common pitfalls.

Example 1

> In my gap year I hope to work and travel.

Comment

This statement is far too vague and would cause many admissions tutors to wonder whether you had really good reasons for deferring entry, or whether you were just postponing the decision to take up a place on their course.

Example 2

> In my gap year I hope to travel to gain work experience.

Comment

This is likely to lead to questions such as: What kind of work experience? For how long? Is it relevant to your chosen course? How? Where? What will you do while you are there? Try to be as specific as possible. This candidate's statement would have been better if they had explained what sort of work experience they wanted and what drew them to their chosen country.

Mature students

You should say something about what you have done since leaving school. If, like many mature applicants, you are rather older and have had a variety of occupations and experience, you may find the Apply screens too restrictive. In this case you can, if you wish, summarise your career and then send a full CV direct to your chosen institutions (not to UCAS). However, there is enough space for you to present your background and interests in a fair amount of detail.

Everyone's circumstances are different, but the following example is the kind of thing that might attract favourable attention from an admissions tutor.

Example

> - 1990: Left school aged 16, no qualifications.
> - 1991–94: Various periods of travel, manual work and unemployment.
> - 1994–2002: RAF (included technical training).

- 2002–2016: Self-employed (motor repairs).
- 2016–18: Access course, Silverbridge College (full time) with a view to entering law school.

Most of my experience has been in manual trades, but I now think I have the ability to change direction. I have known many people who have taken degrees and I think I can make a success of it.

My interest in law was awakened by a friend's problem over an insurance claim. I tried to help her and started exploring the law books in the library. I realised that this was an intellectual challenge I could relate to.

Since then I have done more reading and visited the courts. I have started to help in the Citizens' Advice Bureau. Now I want to qualify and I hope to work in a Community Law Centre. My non-academic interests include travel (in various countries), motor car restoration and socialising.

TIP!

Make sure that your statement is all your own work. UCAS will use similarity detection software to check your statement against other statements. If they detect similarity they will inform the universities and colleges that you have applied to. They will also let you know. Each of your universities and colleges will decide independently what action to take.

18 | Finishing off

Declaration

The declaration can be found under the 'Send to referee' section of Apply. Once you have completed all sections of Apply, you need to read the declaration carefully, only agreeing if you are absolutely sure that you are happy with its contents. UCAS cannot process your application unless you confirm your agreement with its terms and conditions, which legally binds you to make the required payment (see page 161).

When you submit your application, there is no need to sign anything by hand: ticking the relevant boxes and clicking on the 'I agree' button suffices.

Remember: by agreeing you are saying that the information you have provided is accurate, complete and all your own work and that you agree to abide by the rules of UCAS. You are also agreeing to your personal data being processed by UCAS and institutions under the relevant data protection legislation. Any offer of a place you may receive is made on the understanding that, in accepting it, you also agree to abide by the rules and regulations of the institution.

To prevent and detect fraud of any nature, UCAS may have to give information about you to other organisations, including the police, the Home Office, the Foreign and Commonwealth Office, UK Visas and Immigration, the Student Loans Company, local authorities, the SAAS, examination boards or awarding bodies, the Department for Work and Pensions and its agencies and other international admissions organisations.

If UCAS or an institution has reason to believe that you or any other person has omitted any mandatory information requested in the instructions on Apply, has failed to include any additional material information, has made any misrepresentation or given false information, UCAS and/ or the institution will take whatever steps it considers necessary to establish whether the information given in your application is correct.

UCAS and the institutions reserve the right at any time to request that you, your referee or your employer provide further information relating to any part of your application, e.g. proof of identity, status, academic qualifications or employment history. If such information is not provided within the time limit set by UCAS, UCAS reserves the right to cancel your application. Fees paid to UCAS in respect of applications that are cancelled as a result of failure to provide additional information as requested, or as a result of providing fraudulent information, are not refundable.

False information is defined as including any inaccurate or omitted examination results. Omission of material information will include failure to complete correctly the declaration on the application relating to criminal convictions and failure to declare any other information that might be significant to your ability to commence or complete a course of study.

Submitting your application

Once you have agreed to the terms of the declaration, you can pass your application on to your UCAS coordinator or administrator, who will usually be a head of sixth form, form teacher or careers adviser.

They will then check it over, add your reference (see page 162), make arrangements for collecting your application fee and, finally, send it to UCAS.

If you find that you need to alter your application after you have submitted it, you should ask your UCAS coordinator or administrator to return it to you. You will then be able to make the necessary changes before resubmitting it. If mistakes are spotted by the coordinator or administrator, they will return it to you for amendments.

Payment

Application to higher education via UCAS costs £24 (or £18 if you apply to only one course).

If you are making your application through your school or college, it will let you know how it handles payments. (Normally you will pay by debit or credit card, but some schools and colleges prefer to collect individual applicants' fees themselves and send UCAS a single payment covering everyone.) If you are not making your application through a school or college, you will need to make your payment via the internet using a credit or debit card.

You do not need to make your payment until you have completed your application. Once you have agreed to the terms of use of the Apply system in the declaration, you will be asked for your card details (if you are paying by this method). Apply will automatically know whether you should pay the full £24 or the single-choice fee of £18. UCAS accepts UK and international Visa, Visa Electron, Delta, MasterCard, JCB and Maestro credit and debit cards. At the moment it does not accept American Express or Diners Club cards. The card you use to pay need not be in your own name, but you will require the consent of the cardholder.

If you are applying as an individual but your old school or college has agreed to supply your reference, you can send your application to it. Your school or college will then return it to you with the reference attached for you to submit the application directly to UCAS and make your payment.

Reference

The good news is that you are not allowed to write your own reference, so there is relatively little for you to do here. Your referee (usually a teacher, if you are applying via a school or college) will write it and then attach it to your application, through the UCAS coordinator or administrator.

Having said this, it is important not to disregard your reference entirely. In some ways it is the most important item in the selection process. It is only your referee who can tell the admissions tutors about your attitude and motivation, and who can comment on your ability, so admissions tutors are not reliant solely on the exam results and information about exams to be taken that you provide elsewhere in your application.

Points of particular concern to admissions tutors include:

- academic achievement and potential
- suitability and motivation for the chosen course
- predicted grades
- personal qualities
- career aspirations
- mitigating circumstances (such as illness or bereavement) that may have adversely affected a student's performance in previous examinations.

Referees are asked to estimate your level of performance in forthcoming exams, and these predictions of likely grades are important to your chances of acceptance. The best advice, in this respect, is to work hard and impress your referee! Under the Data Protection Act 1998, you have the right to see your reference. You should contact UCAS if you want to see all the information UCAS holds about you, including what your referee has written about you. There is now no such thing as a confidential reference.

Your reference will normally come from your present school or college, or the school or college you attended most recently. If you choose anyone else, make sure it is someone who can provide the kind of assessment higher education institutions need. Be aware that, if you are attending a school or college, it will look very odd if you choose some-one from outside as your referee.

What happens next?

On receipt of your application, UCAS will (usually within 24 hours) send out a welcome email containing your Personal ID and a copy of the list of your higher education course choices in random order. You should check this thoroughly and contact UCAS immediately if anything is incorrect.

You can use your Personal ID to log in to Track in order to follow the progress of your application. Later in the application cycle you will receive instructions from UCAS that will help you to conclude a successful higher education application. For more information on this and on offers, see Part II of this book.

19| Troubleshooting

Some common problems

I can't log in ...

If your buzzword or password does not seem to be working, check the following.

- Have you entered the password correctly? Login details are case sensitive, so check that you have all the characters exactly right.
- Are you in the student area (not the staff area, which is for your referee)?
- Is your computer properly connected to the internet?
- Are you able to connect to other websites?

If the answer to all of these questions is 'Yes', you may have a problem with your network or internet service provider. Try connecting to the main UCAS site, www.ucas.com – if you can, there may be a problem with Apply and you should call UCAS' Contact Centre on 0871 468 0 468.

I've forgotten my username/password ...

If you forget your username or password at any time, click on 'Forgotten login?' and enter the email address you provided on your application. UCAS will send you a reminder of your username and a link to reset your password.

Once you have successfully logged in, you can change your password, your security questions or language preference by clicking on 'Options/ Opsiynau' to the left of the screen.

I'm locked out ...

If you attempt to log in five times without success, for whatever reason, your account will automatically be locked. To regain access, you can:

- ask the UCAS coordinator or administrator at your centre to unlock your account and/or help create a new password for you
- call the UCAS Customer Experience Centre for help on 0371 468 0 468
- wait for 24 hours – after which you will be able to try again.

If you close the internet browser window in which Apply is sitting, rather than exiting by logging out, and you attempt to log back in, you will be presented with the message: 'You are already logged in. Please ensure this is your only active session.' Click 'Log in' if you wish to proceed. This is to protect against your application being open on more than one device at the same time. If you click on 'Log in' you will be allowed back into your account.

> **TIP!**
>
> If you leave Apply open without touching it, it will time out for security reasons and you will have to log in again.

I've pasted my statement into Apply and it's all gone wrong ...

The default character size for statements in Apply is 12 point. If you have written your personal statement in Word and used a larger font size, it might not fit when you try to paste it into Apply.

You may lose formatting when you paste your personal statement into Apply – you should edit your statement very carefully. You will not be able to use bold or italicised fonts. The character and line count in Apply may be different from those in your word-processing package. This is because formatting characters, such as paragraphs, are counted in Apply but may not be counted in Word or Pages.

I've completed my application and sent it to my referee, but now I want to make a change to it ...

You'll have to email or personally contact your referee, who can send the document back to you to amend.

> **TIP!**
>
> It's a good idea if you and your group's UCAS coordinator or administrator develop an email system for alerting individuals that their application has been returned to them for amendment and that they can unlock it again to make the necessary changes. This system can work both ways!

More trouble to shoot?

Once you start completing your application, you can find help on each screen of Apply. Most difficulties can be sorted out quickly by clicking on the 'Help' icon and following the clear instructions.

And finally ...

If you feel you need more information on the application process, visit the website, www.ucas.com.

Glossary

Apply
UCAS' on-line application system. You use this to apply to universities and colleges.

BMAT
A test used by some universities in selecting applicants for medicine.

CV
Curriculum vitae: a document giving details of your qualifications and experience.

Careerscape
A website that can help students to choose higher education courses and careers: https://careerscape.cascaid.co.uk.

Centigrade
A program to help students to decide on suitable higher education courses: www.centigradeonline.co.uk.

Clearing
A service run by UCAS in the summer after all the advanced results are known, to match applicants without places with universities and colleges that still have vacant places.

eCLIPS
Careers information online: www.eclips-online.co.uk.

Erasmus
The EuRopean Community Action Scheme for the Mobility of University Students enables students to study for at least three months or undertake an internship for a period of at least two months at one of more than 4,000 higher education institutions in a European country. Students do not pay extra tuition fees to the university that they attend and can apply for an Erasmus grant to help cover the additional expense of living abroad. It is not yet known whether the UK will continue to participate in the programme after Brexit; however, non-EU members Iceland and Norway take part. www.erasmusprogramme.com.

Extra
A chance to make further applications in the spring for applicants who do not get any offers of places or do not accept any offers from their initial applications.

Graduate
Someone who has a degree.

Higher Ideas
A program to help students to decide on suitable higher education courses: www.careersoft.co.uk/Products/Higher_Ideas.

Job Explorer Database
Careers information online: www.careersoft.co.uk/Products/Job_Explorer_Database.

LNAT
A test used by some universities in selecting applicants for law.

Morrisby Careers Questionnaire
A program to help students to decide on suitable higher education courses: www.morrisby.com.

Postgraduate
Someone studying on an advanced degree course e.g. an MA or MSc.

Sandwich course
A degree or diploma course that includes work experience.

Seminar
A discussion in a small group of students, often, but not always, following a lecture on the same topic.

Tariff
The UCAS Tariff is used to allocate points to post-16 qualifications, such as A levels, Highers, BTEC qualifications and others, making it easier for universities and colleges to compare applicants. Universities and colleges may use it when making offers to applicants.

Track
When you have sent your application to UCAS you will receive a Personal ID. You can use this to log in to Track and see how your application is progressing.

Tutorial
A discussion between a much smaller group of students than in a seminar (sometimes just one student) and a lecturer.

UKCAT
A test used by some universities in selecting applicants for medicine.

Undergraduate
A student on a first degree course, eg BA, BSc.

Appendix: A note for staff on Apply

The online UCAS application system, developed over the last few years, affords real benefits both to student applicants and UCAS coordinators or administrators in schools, colleges and careers centres. Apply is a secure area of the UCAS website and no installation is necessary.

Students can use Apply to complete online UCAS applications at school, home or anywhere with internet access. When they have finished, they can send their applications to you for checking and to have references added, before you submit their applications to meet the relevant UCAS deadline.

The Apply system has dramatically reduced the number of errors made by applicants, as they can access online help at every stage of completing their applications. Poor handwriting is consigned to the past. It is possible for personal statements to be checked and revised a number of times, as the information can easily be amended and kept up-to-date.

Apply also allows great flexibility in the mode of payment chosen by the centre. The fee payment method is variable and can be changed through the cycle of the UCAS application process.

You can find out more about registering as a UCAS centre at www.ucas.com/becomeacentre.

Notes for UCAS correspondents

Once you've registered as a UCAS centre, as the UCAS correspondent, you will be emailed a unique centre username and password for the next UCAS application cycle. This will be in May each year. You should make sure UCAS has up-to-date contact details for your school and college by emailing schools@ucas.ac.uk.

You can then log in and enter your name, details of your organisation and a unique buzzword of between six and 30 letters and numerals chosen by you, for use by your applicants. The buzzword identifies your centre to UCAS and will enable applicants to link through your centre to register with Apply.

During registration, students are given a unique username. After registration students enter your buzzword to link their application to your centre. You should write down your buzzword and keep it safe for use during the application cycle. Each applicant chooses a password and four security questions.

As the UCAS corespondent, you will be in charge of staff set-up – registering appropriate staff with individual usernames and passwords. It is a simple task to remove, change or register new staff with different levels of administrative access (permissions).

From the main staff area you can access the following areas.

- **Applications**: shows all the applications being made from your centre, enabling you to view applications and check the progress of individual applications before they are sent to UCAS.
- **References**: where references can be written, read and approved.
- **Link applications to centre:** some applicants register as individuals when they should have registered through your centre. These applicants can ask to be linked to your centre and those who make this request are listed in this section. You can choose whether or not to set up a link.
- **Send to UCAS**: where you can check the status of applications sent to the staff area, methods of payment, individual applicant fees, dates when applications were sent to UCAS and students' Personal IDs.
- **Delete applications**: where you can delete an applicant's record if it is no longer required.
- **Security**: where it is possible to change students' passwords, and where accounts can be unlocked after unsuccessful login attempts.
- **Set-up**: containing all the standard details, your buzzword, chosen method(s) of payment and dates when your centre's applicants will be unavailable for interview, and where you can also register staff members' details and change their permissions.
- **Adviser Track**: all schools and colleges on the UCAS mailing list are invited to subscribe to Adviser Track, which shows your applicants' progress after their applications have been sent to UCAS. Adviser Track gives you access to Applicant Status Reports which allow you to track your students' progress throughout the application cycle.
- **Options/Opsiynau**: where you can change the language presented in Apply to Welsh or back to English.

The Apply system is a useful administrative tool that can significantly cut the time spent by staff on the annual cycle of UCAS applications.

It is worth gaining the support of senior management to introduce Apply and to train other staff in its use. UCAS offers one-day training sessions for centre staff managing the Apply process. More information about training can be found on the UCAS website at www.ucas.com/advisers/guides-and-resources/training.